Orkney

Entire History, Historical Sites, Historical Events, People and Tradition.

Author
Kingsley Foster

Copyright Notice

Copyright © 2017 Global Print Digital
All Rights Reserved

<u>Digital Management Copyright Notice</u>. This Title is not in public domain, it is copyrighted to the original author, and being published by **Global Print Digital**. No other means of reproducing this title is accepted, and none of its content is editable, neither right to commercialize it is accepted, except with the consent of the author or authorized distributor. You must purchase this Title from a vendor who's right is given to sell it, other sources of purchase are not accepted, and accountable for an action against. We are happy that you understood, and being guided by these terms as you proceed. Thank you

First Printing: 2017.

ISBN: 978-1-912483-12-9

Publisher: Global Print Digital.
Arlington Row, Bibury, Cirencester GL7 5ND
Gloucester
United Kingdom.
Website: www.homeworkoffer.com

Table of Content

Introduction 9
History 12
   The Mesolithic c9000-4000BC 13
   The Neolithic 4000-1800BC 14
   The Bronze Age 1800-800BC 15
   The Iron Age 800BC-500AD 18
      The Riddle of the Iron Age Dead 20
      Religion and belief 20
   The Picts 300-800AD 21
   The Norse Takeover 23
   Pawned to Scotland 24
   Prehistoric Sites 25
      Prehistoric Monuments 25
         Standing Stones and Megaliths 25
            Orkney's Standing Stones 25
            The Ring of Brodgar, Stenness 27
            The Standing Stones of Stenness 46
            The Odin Stone 54
            The Watchstone, Stenness 56
            The Yetnasteen, Rousay 58
            The Stane o' Quoybune, Birsay 59
            The Barnhouse Stone, Stenness 61
            The Deepdale Stone, Stromness 62
            The Stan Stane, North Ronaldsay 64
            The Stone o' Setter, Eday 64
         Burial Chambers and Cairns 66
            Orkney's Chambered Cairns 66
            Maeshowe 68
            The Isbister Cairn The Tomb of the Eagles 71
            The Bookan Chambered Cairn, Sandwich 72
            The Cuween Hill Cairn, Firth 74
            The Dwarfie Stane, Hoy 76
            The Crantit Cairn, St Ola 79
            The Wideford Hill Cairn 80
            The Quoyness Cairn, Sanday 82
            The Unstan Cairn, Stenness 83
            The Blackhammer Cairn, Rousay 85
            The Taversoe Tuick, Rousay 86
            The Knowes of Trotty 88

Settlements and Dwellinghouses 92
    The Stonehall Neolithic Settlement 92
    The Knap o' Howar, Papay 95
    Skara Brae 97
    The Barnhouse Neolithic Settlement 99
    The Ring of Bookan, Sandwick 101
Iron Age Orkney 102
    Minehowe The Underground Enigma 102
    Orkney's Underground 'Earth-houses' 104
    Orkney's Brochs 105
Holy Sites 107
    Eynhallow The Holy Isle 107
    The Brough of Deerness 109
    St Magnus Kirk, Egilsay 112
    St Olaf's Kirk, Kirkwall 113
    The Orphir Round Kirk 114
    The Brough of Birsay 115
    St Magnus Cathedral, Kirkwall 123
Ancient Towns 126
    Stromness The Haven Bay 126
    Kirkwall Orkney's Capital 127
Castles and Strongholds 130
    The Brough of Birsay 130
    Cubbie Roo's Castle, Wyre 131
    The Bishop's Palace, Kirkwall 133
    The Earl's Palace, Birsay 135
    The Earl's Palace, Kirkwall 136
    Noltland Castle, Westray 138
Archaeological Finds 141
    The Skaill Viking Hoard 141
    Norse Hogback Tombstones 143
    The Scar Viking Boat Burial 143
    The Groatsetter Bronze Age Sword 146
    The Orkney Hood 148
    The "Orkney Venus" 150
Characters in Orcadian History 152
    Earl Sigurd and the Raven Banner 152
    The Conversion of Earl Sigurd 155
    Earl Thorfinn the Mighty 156
    Magnus the Martyr of Orkney 160
    Earl Harald and the Poison Shirt 161

- Kolbein Hruga The original Cubbie Roo? 163
- Sweyn Asleifsson 'The Ultimate Viking' 164
- Earl Sigurd the Powerful 168

Events in Orkney's History 170
The Viking Days of the Earldom 170
- The Death of King Haakon 170
- Earl Harald and the Poison Shirt 173
- Magnus the Martyr of Orkney 174

Scottish Rule 176
- The Battle of Summerdale 176

The Sixteenth Century 179
- The Westray Dons and the Spanish Armada 179

The Seventeenth Century 182
- The Covenanters and the Crown 182

Early Historical References to Orkney 184

People, Culture and Tradition 186
Tradition 186
Annual Festivities 186
- The Festival of the Horse and Boys' Ploughing Match 186
- The Kirkwall Ba' 187
- Yule The Midwinter Festival 190
- Orkney's Harvest Lore 192
- Gyro Night 193
- Orcadian Bonfire Traditions 195
- A Year of Orcadian Tradition 197

Charms and Healing 207
- Holy Wells and Magical Waters 207
- Dian-stanes and "Thunderstones" 210
- The Charm of the 'Wreestin' Threed' 212

Language and Custom 213
- About the Orkney Islands 213
- Norn the Language of Orkney 215
- Orkney's 'Teu Neems' 217
- Orkney Placenames 217

Other Traditions 219
- Eynhallow The Holy Isle 219
- Kelp Burning in Orkney 220
- Darraðarljoð The Battle Song of the Valkyries 222
- Orkney and the Arthurian Legends 226
- The Eternal Battle 228
- Odin in Orkney tradition 230

- Magnus the Martyr of Orkney 231
- The Westray Dons and the Spanish Armada 233

The Stages of Life 236
- Orcadian Childbirth Traditions 236
- Marriage Divinations 239
- Orcadian Wedding Traditions 242
- Orcadian Wedding Traditions 243
- The Customs of Death 245

Introduction

Orkney consists of a group of over 70 islands and skerries, of which about 20 are presently inhabited. Lying at approximately 59°N and 3°W, the islands lie just north of Scotland, the shortest distance being about 10km (6 miles) from Caithness, and cover an area of 974 km^2 (376 miles^2), of which the Mainland comprises about half.

Inhabited by 21,350 people (1991 census), the islands are about 85km (53 miles) from north to south and 37km (23 miles) from east to west. The main island is known as the "Mainland", and has three-quarters of the population, as well as the main towns, Kirkwall (population 7,445), and Stromness (population 2,175).

Although apparently isolated, the islands are very well served for communications with Scotland. The MV *St Ola* (3,039 tons, 500 passengers, 180 cars) runs daily between Stromness and Scrabster (often several times per day), while MV *St Sunniva* (4,211 tons, 407 passengers, 120 cars) runs between Orkney, Aberdeen and Shetland. There is also a summer passenger ferry between John O'Groats and Burwick, as well as several freight services. There are frequent daily air links with Wick, Aberdeen, Inverness and Edinburgh, as well as with Shetland by British Airways Express (Loganair).

The earliest written reference to Orkney is by the Greek explorer, Pytheas, from Marseilles, who may have circumnavigated Orkney about the year 325 BC, and claimed to have sighted the edge of the world, or *Ultima Thule*. He was probably seeing Foula, or another part of Shetland to the North. Claudius' fleet is said to have formed a treaty with the Orcadians in AD 43, and Tacitus mentions that a Roman fleet subdued Orkney after the battle of Mons Graupius in AD 83. These references are interesting, but probably not very reliable.

Orkney is referred to in the *Anglo-Saxon Chronicle*, the *Irish Annals* and by various writers such as Adomnan, but it is not until the Norse sagas, written in the 12th century, that we find more recent history. These sagas were written some time after the events so colourfully described, and thus may be of dubious historical accuracy in parts, but nevertheless they give a vivid and graphic account of the Norse age. Being so fertile, and so near to Norway, Orkney was an obvious base for Viking expansion, particularly in a time when the latest technology was sea transport in Viking longships.

In more recent times Orkney has been visited by a large number of eminent people many of whom have written in various terms about our islands. We also have a number of distinguished local authors, and for those wishing further reading, there is always a good selection of books available in the local book shops. For reference the Orkney Library also has an excellent "Orkney Room", which has a very wide range of literature on Orkney. Many books which are unfortunately "out of print" are available for consultation in this room.

The purpose of this Guide is to help visitors to our islands appreciate Orkney and enjoy their time here to the full. The idea is that the reader can assimilate information without effort and yet rapidly find out what he or she would most like to see and do, depending on interest, season or weather. There are so many things to see and do in Orkney that a lifetime is not long enough!

Although we have a beautiful landscape, history everywhere, and wildlife to rival anywhere on Earth, there is another aspect of Orkney which is perhaps the most important and rewarding to get to know the Orcadians themselves. The Orcadians are a friendly, hospitable people, mindful and respectful of their past and at the same time very go-ahead and industrious. Do not hesitate to ask the way, or about things you are sure to get a courteous reply, and if you are lucky you might get a few good stories as well!

History

History of the Orkney Islands

The Orkney Islands have a long and colourful history. It is no exaggeration to say that the isles are a place where this history remains a part of everyday life.

Every corner of the islands has its ancient monuments, most of them in a remarkable state of repair. For thousands of years, people have lived and worked in Orkney.

From the stone age Orcadians, who left a legacy of monuments that continue to inspire today, through to the Vikings, who took the islands in the ninth century and made them the centre of a powerful Earldom and part of the kingdom of Norway, and beyond.

The Orkney islands are covered with monuments that stand as constant reminders of the events and people that have gone before.

Houses and tombs dating back 5,000 years share the landscape with Bronze Age cemeteries, standing stones, 2,000 year old brochs, viking ruins, medieval churches and Renaissance palaces.

Our history is therefore not something that exists only in schoolbooks, or in the thoughts of academics. Orkney's history and heritage is everywhere an intricate tapestry of events stitched into the very fabric of the islands themselves. Orcadians have a connection with this history events that were witnessed by their ancestors many generations ago. The past is alive and remains part of everyday life, albeit unconsciously.

The Mesolithic c9000-4000BC

Compared to the wealth of material for later periods of prehistory, the evidence of the human inhabitants of Orkney during the Mesolithic period is scant.

The people of the Mesolithic were nomadic hunter-gatherers, living in small groups and shifting according the season and the availability of food supplies. This, along with the fact that they did not leave stone constructions such as Skara Brae or Maeshowe, means that they have left little trace for the modern archaeologist.

Although we know that these wandering hunters crossed from Scotland into Orkney, it was not clear when, until the discovery of a charred hazelnut shell in 2007. The shell was recovered during the excavations at Longhowe, in Tankerness, and was carbon dated to 6820-6660 BC, showing that people were in the islands around 7,000 BC, some time after the ice sheets had retreated north and the climate improved.

At this time, however, the wooded landscape of Orkney would have been unrecognizable to modern Orcadians. The sea-level was considerably lower up to 30 metres lower so today's green, rolling Orkney hills would have been the peaks of high ground.

What the Mesolithic hunters would have regarded as lowland areas are now under metres of water a fact that goes some way to explains the lack of archaeological evidence.

Whenever they arrived in Orkney, it is doubtful that they settled in one place for any length of time. Their survival depended on hunting and gathering food, so when one supply ran out they moved elsewhere. As a result, they left no tangible buildings or objects, other than a handful of stone flakes, as evidence of their movement.

Instead, they existed much as the nomadic cultures of the world still do today living in temporary shelters that could be easily dismantled and transported between sites.

They lived off the land, gathering roots, berries and shellfish and hunting birds and animals in a land recently emerging from an icy sleep.

The Neolithic 4000-1800BC

The real evidence of Orkney's human history begins to appear at some point before the fourth millennium BC.

By this time the bands of hunter-gatherers of the Mesolithic had gradually evolved into a agricultural society and small communities of farmers were making their way across the Pentland Firth from Caithness and western Scotland to settle in the fertile northern islands.

As farmers, the nomadic lifestyle of the Mesolithic had to cease as the raising of crops required permanent settlements in areas of good soil. But despite the importance of agriculture, the people of the Neolithic still relied on hunting and fishing to survive.

The daily way of life of these early farmers can be gleaned from the remains of their houses, burial places and monuments, as well as the less grand, but equally important, materials such as pottery, tools and refuse.

Places such as the Knap of Howar on Papay and Skara Brae on the western shores of the Orkney Mainland give clear insights into the domestic lives of the farming communities. At the Knap o' Howar, for example, the bones of domesticated cattle, sheep and pigs were found alongside those of wild deer, whales and seals.

Their tradition of elaborate burials within chambered cairns such as Cuween, Widefordand Quanterness also gives tantalising glimpses of these early Orcadians, their beliefs and customs.

Cairns were an essential part of life to the early farmers with men, women and children of all ages buried within the chambered tombs they erected throughout Orkney.

Analysis of the bones found within these tombs tells us of a population in which few people reached the age of 50 and in which those who survived childhood, usually died in their thirties.

Over the years the small farming communities gradually developed into larger tribal units, perhaps with an elite ruling class. These communities were capable of constructing the major tribal monuments such as Maeshowe and the Ring of Brodgar.

From around 2900BC the "heartland" of the Orkney Mainland the area surrounding the lochs of Stenness and Harray was a sacred ceremonial meeting place.

This sacred centre remained important to the people of Orkney for 2000 years until the once-common group burials were replaced by the individual interments common of the Bronze Age.

The Bronze Age 1800-800BC

Towards the end of the third millennium BC, prehistoric society in Orkney saw a number of changes that heralded the arrival of the Bronze Age.

New ideas and concepts were spreading through Britain, the most important of which was the introduction of metal, in particular copper and bronze.

But the changes sweeping southern Britain did not seem to catch on in Orkney, where metal goods remained scarce probably remaining as objects of prestige and power.

Although copper could be found naturally in Orkney, there is a distinct lack of evidence for copper mining in the county. This could imply that metal objects were still being imported and, as such, remained relatively rare, prestigious goods.

The apparent reluctance to embrace the new technologies has been blamed on the ancient Orcadians, who, it has been suggested, were not keen to move away from their old traditions and accept the new. This idea is debatable, however, and in truth there is much still to be learned about Bronze Age Orkney.

But gradually, changes did occur.

Bronze Age construction moved away from the large monumental structures, such as Maeshowe, and although there remains little evidence of Bronze Age settlements, it appears that clustered designs such as Skara Brae were abandoned in favour of individual stone houses in small, dispersed communities.

Burial practices

As people moved away from communal living, they also shifted away from the traditions of communal burial in chambered cairns.

Instead, the practice of individual burials in stone cists, dug into the ground, became more common.

Initially, the dead were buried within their cists but, over time, the practice of cremation found favour, with the cremated remains placed inside the burial cist.

Stone cairns, or earthen mounds, known as barrows, were erected over these cists, which were usually clustered in small groups in certain areas. Fine examples of Orkney barrow burials can be found around the Ring o' Brodgar in Stenness and the Knowes o' Trotty in Harray.

As the chambered cairns fell out of use, they were permanently sealed up and filled in, or in some cases, such as Pierowall, in Westray, destroyed.

This shift in emphasis " from community to individual " hints at a rise of a more hierarchical society, where the individual, a leader, for example, was deemed more important.

Climate deterioration

One change the Bronze Age Orcadians had absolutely no control over was the deterioration in the islands' climate.

During the Bronze Age temperatures dropped and rainfall levels increased changes that made living, and farming, in Orkney difficult.

The islands may also have become more isolated as travel became more hazardous. It has been suggested, in the past, that the climate deterioration and resultant harsh lifestyle may have led to an exodus from the islands. This, it is thought, could explain the lack of Bronze Age remains in Orkney.

However, more recent paleoecological work in the county indicates that there was no major change in human activity in Orkney during the Bronze Age.

Burnt mounds

Burnt mounds are typical of Bronze Age Orkney.

They are generally just mounds of blackened earth, usually found near a source of fresh water, mixed with the remains of heated stones and ash. Beneath these mounds lie the remains of paved areas, usually incorporating a hearth and a stone lined pit.

Burnt mounds are generally agreed to be the remains of areas used for heating water. Stones, which had been heated in fires, were placed in a water-filled tank. The hot stones then heated the water. What this hot water, or steam, was used for depends on which theory you follow.

Some favour the idea that the sites were purely domestic and used for cooking, while others suggest a more ritualistic use, perhaps a sweathouse or sauna.

Whatever the purpose, as the stones cooled and cracked, the remains were discarded and built up around the area, along with quantities of ash, to form the burnt mounds that dot the landscape today.

The presence of low stone walls surrounding many of the structures has prompted some experts to suggest that the structure may have been roofed.

The Iron Age 800BC-500AD

The Iron Age in Orkney, as in the rest of Scotland, seems to have been a time of change and unrest. At the time, the people of Orkney were probably still arranged in fragmented individual tribes, each likely to be under the leadership of an independent 'chieftain'.

Climatic deterioration had begun in the Bronze Age but around 600BC Orkney's climate deteriorated further. The islands became colder and wetter and as peat and heather claimed the once-fertile high ground, upland cultivation became impossible, forcing people down to the low-lying areas.

The shortage of good, fertile soil meant land became precious and the competition for farmland may have led to a more aggressive society. The construction of robust, fortified dwellings in Orkney coincides with the expansion of the bronze industry on the Scottish mainland something that saw a marked increase in the number of readily available weaponry.

These roundhouses began appearing from around 600BC, and by 100BC had evolved into the massive, fortified stone towers we now know as brochs.

Although there is no denying their defensive properties, it may be that the roundhouse and broch were as much a visible symbol of social status than a fortress or refuge.

Around 120 brochs have been recorded in Orkney, but whether they were actually intended for defence, or were merely a symbol of wealth and prestige, the popularity of the monumental broch declined in importance around 100AD.

Orcadian society in the Iron Age had formed into distinct social layers with an "aristocratic" ruling class above the ordinary islander. As in more recent history, a substantial and impressive dwelling was a good way to mark territory and remind others of the individual's standing in the community.

Throughout the Iron Age, metal goods were being crafted in Orkney, with the metalworking at Minehowe in Tankerness being hailed as one of one of the best assemblages of Iron Age metalworking in Britain. Together with this industry, there appears to have been an extensive series of trading routes in operation.

During the Iron Age, Orkney was far from isolated, with discoveries of Roman pottery and artefacts are a number of broch sites as well as Minehowe in Tankerness. The accounts of Pytheas in 325BC shows that the islands were at least known in the Mediterranean.

The standard of life in Orkney seems to have been quite high. Evidence shows that, by Iron Age standards, Orkney was a prosperous and secure place.

This prosperity was the result of mixed farming activities combined with fishing and hunting. Grain was grown but farming centred around the rearing of cattle thus providing not only meat and milk but also leather pigs, sheep, hens and goats. The broch builders also hunted, though this was not only through necessity but for leisure.

By the 4th and 5th centuries AD, patterns of farming had changed in Orkney. Its Iron Age tribes had become part of the Pictish nation. They lived in farmsteads across the Orcadian landscape one shamrock-shaped farm being built right next to the Broch of Gurness.

The Riddle of the Iron Age Dead

The Iron Age 700BC-500AD

Although there is ample evidence about how the people of the Iron Age lived, one area that remains clouded in uncertainty what did they do with their dead?

In contrast to the vast amount known about Neolithic funerary custom, when it comes to the Iron Age a lack of physical evidence has left this area vague.

Recent archaeological work in Orkney, particularly at Minehowe in Tankerness, andthe Knowe o' Skea in Westray, is shedding more light on the subject, but there is still a lot not known.

Some excavations have revealed burials in stone cists, where others have shown bodies (or body parts) were "built" into houses the walls, for example, or under the floor.

At Minehowe in Tankerness, for example, a woman was found buried under the floor of an Iron AGe metalworking structure, while at Howe, outside Stromness, a body was found to have been left in a disused building.
In short, there is still much to be learned about this subject.

Religion and belief

Like funerary custom, a lack of evidence means that there is little we can say for certain about the religious beliefs of the Iron Age

Orcadians. However, from discoveries made at brochs and past work at Minehoweand the Knowe o' Skea, as well as evidence from other areas of Scotland, we can make some suppositions.

Fragments of the beliefs of Iron Age Orkney probably survived, to a certain extent, in some of the customs and traditions of Orkney. For example, the Iron Age inhabitants of the isles probably believed in a number of gods, or spirits, who affected their everyday lives in various different ways from calming storms to working metals, from ensuring bountiful crops to protecting the household.

In the Iron Age, it would appear the people had a particular affinity to water particularly springs, pools or lochs. In Orkney, as well as throughout the British Isles, we have evidence of artefacts being ritually thrown into bodies of water, presumably as offerings of some sort.

These water-logged discoveries are borne out by the Roman accounts which confirm that the people of north-western Europe revered bodies of water, considering them to be "gateways" to their gods. These customs appear to have been present in Orkney, with a number of spectacular items found in areas of marshy ground in Tankerness.

These water-cults may also have had some connection to the "wells" found in a number of brochs, most notably Gurness, and, of course, the underground chamber of Minehowe.

The Picts 300-800AD

From the writings of the classical authors who mention northern Britain, we know that by the fourth century AD the Picts known to the Romans as "Picti" or "Painted People" were the predominant force in northern Scotland.

Orkney was, at least for a time, part of this Pictish Kingdom, probably with its own local ruler, but owing fealty to a central High King.

Adomnan, the biographer of St Columbus, states that there were Orcadians at the court of the Pictish High King, Bridei, in 565 AD. These Orcadians were described as "hostages" which could imply that relations between Orkney and Pictish King was perhaps strained the hostages being Bridei's insurance policy to keep Orkney on a tight leash. Some historians, however, have pointed out that these 'hostages' could have an altogether less hostile interpretation and that they were merely guests at the King's court.

Although we now think they were simply the descendants of the original broch builders, surprisingly little is known about the Pictish Orcadians. This lack of evidence is due in part to the fact that the Romans, the major chroniclers of early British History, did not make it this far north in any great number. And we must remember that the Romans regarded the northern Picts as little more than savages.

The most typically Pictish items that can still be seen today are the numerous ornately carved symbol stones dotted across northern Scotland. The meaning of these symbol stones is still debated today. Orkney only boasts a handful of these symbol stones, the most famous being the one found on the The Brough of Birsay, an offshore island settlement on the west coast of the Orkney Mainland. The Brough is known to have been a Pictish site before the Norsemen claimed it for their own.

Orkney's first contact with the new religion of Christianity was more than likely in the sixth century but the islands can not said to have been under church authority until the eighth century.

It was at an even later date that the islands could be said to be totally "Christianised" we must remember that the successors to the Picts were the pagan Norsemen some of whom were reluctant to give up the ways of their forefathers.

The fate of Orkney's Picts remains a controversial question to this day. Were they completely obliterated by the settling Vikings or did the two live together in peaceful co-existence. There are supporters in both camps and the question remains hotly debated.

The Norse Takeover

The Norsemen began to colonise Orkney in the eighth century AD and before long the islands became a vital link in their western sea-routes.

Exactly how the Norse takeover of Orkney took place remains a hotly debated subject to this day. Was it a peaceful integration or did the Norsemen wipe out the indigenous population?

Whatever the circumstances, by the end of the ninth century the Norwegian settlement was firmly established and Orkney's culture and way of life was entirely that of a Norse earldom an earldom that became a powerful political unit and had considerable impact on the history of Scotland.

The history of the Norse Earls of Orkney is recorded in the *Orkneyinga Saga* which recounts events up until the murder of the last of the Norse Earl in 1231. However, although elements of the saga are historically accurate, it remains a literary work and cannot be accepted as entirely trustworthy.

According to the saga, Norway's first noteworthy dealings with Orkney involved King Harald Harfagre, who set out to deal with renegade Vikings who were using the islands as a base for summer raids on Norway. The Saga states that on this expedition a son of the Norwegian Earl Rognvald of Møre was killed, so to recompense the Earl, King Harald gave him Orkney and Shetland.

The saga account, however, is not backed up by other references and is more than likely a 13th century Icelandic "creation", based on their traditions that it was the tyranny of Harald Fairhair that forced their forebears to leave Norway. For more details, .

Whatever the historical truth, the saga goes on to explain that Earl Rognvald had no interest in the islands so passed them on to his brother, Sigurd. The first earl of Orkney, Sigurd the Mighty was the first in a long line of Norwegian earls who controlled Orkney for the next 600 years.

After the death of Earl John Haraldsson in 1231, the Earldom was passed to the son of the Earl of Angus. Despite this, the islands were still owned by Norway and the Scottish inheritor of the island earldom owed allegiance to the Norwegian Crown.

The period in which Orkney played such a major part in the Western Empire of the Norse is considered by some to have been the islands' Golden Age.

Pawned to Scotland

Following the Battle of Largs, in 1263, and the loss of the Western Isles as a result of the Treaty of Perth, in 1266, Orkney and Shetland were the only part of what is now Scotland to remain in Norwegian hands.

But although the islands were still officially under Norse rule, the control Scottish Earls had over Orkney was on the increase.

This culminated in the appointment of Henry Sinclair, Earl of Roslin to the Earldom in 1379, and heralded changes in the ownership of land and the gradual break-up of the Norse systems of tenure.

The Earldom of Orkney was held for the Norwegian (and later Danish) Crown until 1468, at which time the impoverished Christian I, King of Denmark, Norway and Sweden, gave Orkney to the Scottish Crown as part of a marriage agreement with King James III.

The Scottish king was to marry Christian's daughter, Margaret, and by this agreement Orkney was held as a pledge, redeemable by the payment of 50,000 Rhenish Florins.

At the end of the first year the payment had not been forthcoming so Shetland was pledged for a further 8,000 Florins.

Two years later, Christian had still not made the payment so the Earldom of Orkney and Lordship of Shetland were annexed to the Scottish Crown.

As the years passed, the Scottish influence over the islands grew and gradually the Norse way of life and language slipped away. By the late 17th century the variant of the Norse language of Orkney Norn was spoken only by the inhabitants of one or two remote parishes.

In 1564, Mary Queen of Scots gifted the Royal Estates in Orkney and Shetland to one Robert Stewart her half-brother and natural son of James V. Thus began the tyranny of the Stewart line traditionally hailed as Orkney's darkest years.

Robert Stewart's acquisition, and subsequent "handling" of the islands, was documented as followed:

> "This miscreant, having secured in addition the whole temporal estates of the bishopric by an excambion effected in 1568, and having become Earl of Orkney in 1581, spent the rest of his life with the exception of a short period during which he was imprisoned, partly as a penalty for improper negotiations with Denmark in oppressing the islanders for his own personal advantage."

Prehistoric Sites
Prehistoric Monuments
Standing Stones and Megaliths

Orkney's Standing Stones

The romance of Orkney's past has its memorials in the many great standing stones that thumb the heavens from vantage points all over the islands."

Jutting skywards from Orkney's gentle landscape are a number of ancient standing stones, each a stark reminder of our prehistoric heritage.

First cut from Orkney flagstone and erected before the Egyptians had begun constructing their pyramids, Orkney's stone sentinels have withstood rain, wind and sun for thousands of years.

The reason the ancient Orcadians went to the considerable effort of raising these stone monuments is still unclear. To our modern minds, the society of Neolithic man is difficult to comprehend a society where everyday life, religion and ritual were inextricably linked.

Theories abound as to their purpose astronomical observatories, territorial markers or calendars each specialist having his own personal thoughts on the subject.

Whatever the reason for their construction, they remain every bit as awe inspiring and powerful today as they must have appeared when an active part of the islands' culture.

Although a number of standing stones have inevitably vanished from the landscape over the years pulled down to provide building materials, or simply to clear a field quite a number were untouched by man and are still standing.

The most famous of these stones are within the Ring o' Brodgar and the Standing Stones o' Stenness but these are just the tip of the iceberg.

Most visitors venture no further than the Stenness complexes the heart of prehistoric Orkney which is a pity, because there are a number on the outer islands that deserve a visit.

Away from the Mainland are stones such as the Fingersteen and the Yetnasteen. These megaliths wait the passing of each day, alone and silent, ignorant of the daily coachloads of tourists that flock to view their seemingly grander cousins at Brodgar and Stenness.

Many of the stones, past and present, had their legends attached to them.

The most common by far is the tradition that some of the monoliths come to life on New Year's Eve (Hogmanay) and walk to a nearby body of water where they dip their heads and drink. Others were thought to be giants, trolls or witches, transformed to stone and frozen in time by the rays of the Orkney sun.

Of all the legends and traditions surrounding Orkney's megaliths, those surrounding the now-destroyed Odin Stone were by far the most potent and deep-seated. This holed stone held a particularly special part in the hearts of Orcadians until its destruction in the 19th century.

For more information on Orkney's megalithic monuments, select from one of the links in the right hand menu

The Ring of Brodgar, Stenness

> "The Ring of Brodgar is the finest known truly circular late Neolithic or early Bronze Age stone ring and a later expression of the spirit which gave rise to Maeshowe, Stenness and Skara Brae."

If one iconic site has come to represent Orkney's ancient heritage, it must surely be the Ring of Brodgar.

Part of the Heart of Neolithic Orkney World Heritage Site, the Ring of Brodgar is found in the West Mainland parish of Stenness. It stands on an eastward-sloping plateau on the Ness of Brodgar a thin strip of land separating the Harray and Stenness lochs.

Because the interior of the Ring of Brodgar has never been fully excavated, or scientifically dated, the monument's actual age remains uncertain. However, it is generally assumed to have been erected between 2500 BC and 2000 BC, and was, therefore, the last of the great Neolithic monuments built on the Ness.

The stone ring was built in a true circle, almost 104 metres wide. Although it is thought to have originally contained 60 megaliths, this figure is not based on archaeological evidence. Today, only 27 stones remain.

In contrast to the giant megaliths that make up the Standing Stones of Stenness, the Brodgar stones are much smaller, varying in height from 2.1 metres (7 feet) to a maximum of 4.7 metres (15ft 3in).

With a diameter of 103.6 metres (340 ft), the Brodgar ring is the third largest stone circle in the British Isles. Covering an area of 8,435 square metres (90,790 square feet), it is beaten only by the outer ring of stones at Avebury and the Greater Ring at Stanton Drew in England. Incidentally, the Brodgar ring is exactly the same size as Avebury's two inner rings.

Like the nearby Standing Stones of Stenness, the Ring of Brodgar has been classed as a henge.

Enclosed by a massive rock-cut ditch, it has two entrance causeways, one to the north-west and the other to the south-east. These two causeways differ in size the south-eastern one just over one metre in width, compared to the 3.4m wide north-western causeway.

However, strictly speaking, Brodgar can't be called a henge, because it lacks the external bank of a true henge.

Heart of Neolithic Orkney

Any visitor to the ring will immediately see why the Ness of Brodgar was considered the ideal place to construct such a great ceremonial monument.

The stone circle is practically in the centre of a massive natural "cauldron" formed by the hills of the surrounding landscape. Today, the site is accentuated by the water of the lochs, but that was not always the case. In fact, when the ring was erected, between 2500BC and 200BC, the Stenness loch didn't exist. Instead the area was wet, marshy bog, surrounding pools of water or lochans.

The sea only breached the narrow landbridge at the Brig o' Waithe in Stenness, filling the loch was salt water, around 1500BC 500 to 1,000 years after the ring was built.

The Ring of Brodgar was part of an enormous prehistoric ritual complex that incorporated the Stones o' Stenness, approximately one mile to the south-east, and, probably, the Ring of Bookan to the north-west. A short distance to the east of the Brodgar ring is the solitary standing stone now known as the Comet Stone.

The area surrounding the Ring of Brodgar, and the entire Ness, is rich with archaeology including four massive mounds thought to have been created between 2500 BC and 1500 BC.

Brodgar or Brogar?

When it comes to the Brodgar name it is no wonder the visitor is often confused.

It appears on some maps and accounts as *Brogar* although this actually has no bearing on the "correct" Orcadian pronunciation, which is *broa(d)yeur*, where there is slight emphasis on the "d".

Over the years, particularly outside the West Mainland parishes of Sandwick, Stromness and Stenness, this pronunciation corrupted and it is now more common to hear "broad-gur" or Brodgar, as it is now written.

Recorded in 1563 as "Broager", it seems likely that this local pronunciation led to the gradual inclusion of a "d" when the name came to be written.

In 2004, Historic Scotland, who maintain the site, decided to revert to the Orcadian use of "Brodgar" in all its promotional material a move that was widely welcomed by Orcadians.

Early accounts

The Brodgar ring was first recorded in the early 16th century, in an account of Orkney written by the enigmatic author Jo Ben. His *Descriptio Insularum Orchadiarum* is the oldest surviving account of the Orkney Islands since the transfer to Scotland in 1468.

Jo Ben's identity is unknown, although it has been suggested that he was a priest, a visiting superior or travelling monk, who resided in Orkney around 1529.

Regarding the Ring of Brodgar, Jo Ben wrote:

"[In Stenness] beside the lake are stones high and broad, in height equal to a spear, and in an equal circle of half a mile.

In 1792, the ring contained 18 standing stones, with eight lying prone. But by 1815, an account shows that two more stones had been toppled, leaving only 16 erect.

Then, in 1854, in what was the first detailed account of the stone circle, there were only 13 erect stones, ten complete, but fallen, stones and fragments of 13 more.

The Ring of Brodgar was taken into state care in 1906 and, two years later, most of the fallen stones were placed in what was thought to be their original sockets. Since then two stones have suffered lightning strikes, leaving 27 standing today.

Building the stone circles

Although we can only speculate as to the purpose of stone circles, there is one thing we can say for certain their existence shows, without a shadow of a doubt, that the society responsible for the monuments was sufficiently organised to carry out building projects on a massive scale.

An incredible amount of work went into erecting each stone circle, with recent estimates putting the number of man-hours for the Brodgar and Stenness rings at between 85,000 and 200,000.

This figure shows that the monuments were regarded as significant enough to warrant such an incredible outlay of manpower and time.

Competitive behaviour

According to Professor Colin Richards, who excavated at the Ring of Brodgar in 2008, the idea that one "elite" individual, or group, was responsible for the stone circle's construction can be discounted.

Instead, Professor Richards feels that it was not the completed stone circle that was significant, but rather the physical act of constructing it. The prestige of quarrying, transporting and erecting a fine megalith, he suggested, may have been the driving force behind the development of the monument.

A geological examination of the Brodgar megaliths confirmed that the stones had been brought from different areas across Orkney. These quarries, and the different types of stone obtained from them, may, therefore, represent the different people, or communities, involved in the creation of the stone circle.

The construction, he suggested, might have seen competition between the different prehistoric communities.

"My suggestion is that these communities were quite fiercely competitive. The ring, rather than being this 'harmonious temple structure', that was a joint-effort between different communities, was maybe the site of some really quite competitive behaviour, with the various groups attempting to outdo the other with visible shows of prestige and power.

"Labour, and the deployment of labour, was a visible mark of prestige."

This scenario, said Professor Richards, would see the construction of the ring taking generations it would have grown slowly as the megaliths were brought in.

"The great feat of labour employed in the digging of the ditch provides some insight into just how important this separation was to Neolithic people. From the excavation, it seems they dug a section of the ditch and then they left it. The colours of rock in the ditch in Trench A have been influenced by water logging, so the orange-brown Orkney flagstones gives way to a deep grey-blue near the base of the ditch. Strangely enough, this actually gives the appearance of water standing in the ditch bottom.

"From this evidence, it is quite clear that in the northern area, at least, standing water collected soon after the ditch was dug. This may seem strange, but it is worth remembering that the surrounding ditch was cut to enclose the area of the stone circle and in the Orcadian island world, water surrounded islands and people. Therefore, the use of water to create a division to separate it from the rest of the world was an appropriate strategy employing everyday imagery. They were, I believe, creating an 'island' a symbolic area representing the world they lived in, and a world they knew.

He added: "But, in terms of architecture, the circle may not have been the most significant point in the landscape. This 'island' has two opposed entrances probably to enter and exit the circle. The great ring may have been built around a pre-existing pathway and passing through it may have 'altered' a person's state, a bit like entering a church and moving towards the altar. In this case, the end point of the journey may have been further along the Ness of Brodgar."

Selecting and preparing the site

Before we consider the effort required to quarry and transport the stones themselves, we should first look at the preparation of the site.

We can't say for sure what the builders of the Brodgar and Stenness rings were looking for when they set out to find a location for their monuments, but it seems very likely that the chosen sites were significant to them.

The reasoning behind this is simple. There were undoubtedly easier places to erect a stone circle sites, for example, that did not require the builders to mine through bedrock as part of the construction. The 123-metre diameter ditch that surrounds the Ring of Brodgar, was 7.5 metres deep and is cut from solid rock.

Regarding the Ring of Brodgar, Professor Richards suspects the monument was sited on an existing route across the Ness.

The stone circle has two opposed access causeways probably to enter and exit the monument. Professor Richards feels that passing through the Ring of Brodgar was just one part of a longer "ceremony" involving the entire Ness of Brodgar.

He said: "The great ring may have been built around a pre-existing pathway and passing through it may have "altered" a person's state, a bit like entering a church and moving towards the altar. In this case, the end point of the journey may have been further along the Ness of Brodgar."

Which came first the ditch or the stones?

Were the stones erected before or after the ditch? This is an oft-asked question. In truth, we don't really know.

Over the years, many have assumed the stone must have been first, and then the ditch dug around them. The reason? Efficiency it would have been easier to move the stones into position and erect them before the massive ditch was dug.

The danger here, however, is assuming that the Neolithic constructors wanted to make things easy. The modern mindset is focused on speed and economy of effort in other words, what's the easiest and quickest way of getting a job done.

If Professor Richards' theory is correct, and the construction of the stone circle, rather than the completed monument, was important it could be that the harder the task the more significant the action.

In his paper *Rethinking the great stone circles of Northwest Britain*, Professor Richards explained: "If a graph was drawn through time of the various estimates of numbers of individuals required to drag or move a forty ton megalith, from Atkinson's initial experiments through to more recent attempts, it would show a steady decrease from 640 to 100. Such preoccupation with efficiency has led to numerous reconstructions, each of which attempts to outstrip earlier efforts in terms of a lower number of people necessary to move and erect a stone circle.

"Clearly, this obsession is linked to western industrial concepts of labour, efficiency and profitability, however, when we turn to ethnographic examples of stone dragging and monumental construction we find this whole line of reasoning totally inappropriate.

"Indeed, the exact opposite frequently applies whereby it is the ability to obtain the largest possible labour force which provides an index of the status of the organising or sponsoring group. Yet again, contemporary ideas and assumptions appear to dictate the way construction and labour are understood within archaeology."

Measuring the circle and quarrying the stones

Once the ditch digging was under way, or complete, work probably began stripping away the turf and vegetation covering the enclosure, ready for the outline of the stone ring to be measured and marked out.

Being a perfect circle, Brodgar would have been relatively easy to mark out, presumably using a single length of rope, pegged at the circle's centre.

Prior to the excavations in 2008, it was suggested that a number of the Brodgar megaliths came from encircling ditch. However, the archaeologists are now certain that could not be the case.

Because of the geology of the site, it is impossible that a complete megalith could have been extracted from the ditch without breaking.

So, if they didn't come from the ditch, where were they quarried?

Geological studies of the megaliths have shown that the stone came from a number of different sites. Of these, only the location of one is certain.

Although there are a number of traditional sites in Sandwick that are thought to have been the sources for the Stenness and Brodgar megaliths, the best known is Vestrafiold, a hill north of the Bay o' Skaill, in Sandwick.

There, prone stones can still be seen lying on the hillside to this day and recent work at the site has confirmed that some of the Brodgar megaliths were indeed quarried there.

Comparatively little effort would have had to have gone into shaping the stones as the Vestrafiold rock splits easily into slabs. After being quarried from the hillside, the megaliths were transported the 7.5 miles to the Ness of Brodgar.

Transporting the megaliths

To haul the stones overland from Vestrafiold to the Ness of Brodgar would also have required considerable manpower and effort.

Again, we cannot say for certain how the freshly-quarried stones were moved, but the Brodgar megaliths were undoubtedly easier to transport than their larger Stenness cousins.

The widespread notion that the megaliths were hauled over wooden rollers is possible but this might not have been the best way. Aside from the problem of a lack of wood, the method is not particularly efficient over rough or uneven land.

Instead, could it be that some form sled apparatus, possibly using sections of 'track', was employed to drag the stones slowly across the countryside?

A theory that the stones were transported by water, floated down the Stenness loch, was dealt a blow in April 2008, with the results of environmental coring work in the loch.

It showed that prior to around 1500BC, the Stenness loch didn't exist. Instead the area was wet marshy bog, surrounding pools of water or lochans. Not the best landscape to be dragging massive megaliths through.

Erecting the stones

With the momentous task of quarrying and transporting the megaliths complete, the task of erecting on site would probably have been comparatively easy.

The method used by the prehistoric engineers is open to speculation, but it seems likely that a system of platforms, levers, ropes and pulleys were used raise the stones. Systems that continued to be used in the islands for thousands of years afterwards.

Calculations based on size and weight would indicate that the largest stone in the Brodgar ring would have taken around 20 men to raise, with the same number employed to ensure the monolith remained standing.

Given the estimated population at the time, and the close proximity of settlements, scholar Aubrey Burl suggested that a workforce of around 300 labourers would have been available for the construction of Brodgar.

> "Working an unlikely unionised eight-hour day with no breaks for weekend, hauliers could have dragged the stones to the

site, put them up, dug out the ditch, built up the bank and returned to domestic drudgery within a month."

But although based on solid mathematics, Burl summarises the situation perfectly:

"Mathematically, the computation is immaculate. In terms of prehistoric life, it may be no more than fantasy. And what happened inside the completed arena may rest forever unknown.

The question of the ditch and bank

We know without a shadow of a doubt that the Ring of Brodgar was originally surrounded by the deep circular ditch, typical of a henge monument. Sections of the ditch were excavated in 1973, and again in 2008,

This ditch remains clearly visible today, but having filled in over the millennia, is only a shadow of its former self. It has a diameter of around 123 metres (403 ft) and was originally three metres (9.8 ft) deep and seven metres wide.

Cut into bedrock, it has been estimated that around 4,700 cubic metres (11,000 tonnes) of rock had to be quarried to create the 380 metre long ditch a momentous task previously estimated to have taken 80,000 man-hours.

This is the equivalent of 100 people working ten hours a day, for 80 days. Having seen the depth of the ditch, I wonder if that figure is slightly conservative.

Today, the ditch is much shallower than it was. Despite this, it is still possible, with a little imagination, to stand at the Ring's south-eastern entrance causeway to visualise how the site originally looked.

Bank, or no bank?

Strictly speaking, the Ring of Brodgar is not a henge monument. Because there is no evidence of an external bank, the monument does not fit into the classification of a henge.

There is no trace of any bank today something which would be unlikely if the bank was, as has been suggested by some, constructed from the rock quarried from the ditch.

In addition, the fact that the South Knowe was constructed so close to the ditch makes the presence of a bank unlikely. If there had been one there, the knowe would have been built on top of it.

However, given that both the Standing Stones of Stenness and Maeshowe both had encircling banks, some contest that Brodgar was the same.

The purpose of the ditch and bank, if it existed is not completely understood, although it is commonly accepted that the monument had a ritual, or ceremonial, purpose. With this in mind, the ditch/bank probably marked the enclosed area as "special", or sacred.

However, theories abound, with some suggesting that any bank kept the ceremonies held within the ring "private" while others feel that it may have had some function in the site's use as an astronomical observatory.

The Surrounding Archaeology

Although the megaliths on the Ness of Brodgar are the most striking remains of Orkney's ancient past, they are but the tip of the archaeological iceberg.

The landscape surrounding the Ring of Brodgar, and the nearby Standing Stones of Stenness, is littered with archaeological sites many of which go unnoticed by visitor and local alike.

The Brodgar ring, for example, is surrounded by a complex of Bronze Age burial barrows, mounds, cairns and prehistoric earthworks.

The most visible of these, the four mounds now known as Salt Knowe, Fresh Knowe, South Knowe and Plumcake Knowe, were excavated in the early 19th century.

The significance of the landscape

Although there are several visible sites, a comprehensive geophysics scanning project on the entire Ness of Brodgar revealed that the entire peninsula is covered in anomalies.

These indicate that the area was once the site of considerable human activity.

But these scans have also shown that the area immediately surrounding the Ring of Brodgar seems to have been regarded "differently" by those who lived on the Ness.

The scans revealed considerable activity from the Standing Stones of Stenness right up to current Brodgar Farm. At this point, however, from a landscape rife with anomalies, there comes an almost clinically-defined line where activity ceases. A distinct cut off-point that perhaps marks an invisible boundary the area's inhabitants did not want to cross.

Does this mark the start of a symbolic shift in the perception of the landscape?

Or is there a more mundane reason? A field or territorial boundary perhaps?

The same pattern is repeated to the north of the ring, with a cut-off point that seems to demarcate the ritual area around the stone circle. Here, the boundary seems to be marked by an earthen bank that runs across the Ness.

The Dyke o' Sean

The Dyke o' Sean (pronounced "see-ahn") is a huge earthwork that crosses the Ness of Brodgar from east to west.

Up to seven metres wide in parts, and up to a metre high, the man-made earthwork snakes across the landscape from the Stenness loch to the Harray loch.

These days, the Dyke o' Sean marks the boundary between the parishes of Stenness and Sandwick but its age has never been determined. But in light of the new geophysics data, it seems possible that the Dyke o' Sean is contemporary with the Brodgar ring, perhaps marking an outer boundary on the northern edge of the Brodgar henge complex.

A tantalising reference to a "dilapidated dyke" to the south of the ring, on a mid-19th century map of the Ness, could indicate a similar earthwork.

So within these boundaries, the land around the Ring of Brodgar seems to have been maintained as a definite "non domestic" area a space set apart from "everyday" life and perhaps connected with the ritual or religious practices centred on the stone circle.

Or was the area around the ring perceived as being distinctly different and as such avoided?

What was it used for?

"..a common theory has been that they had some connection with the religion of the Druids, and may have been places of sacrifice."
J. Gunn Orkney the Magnetic North (1932)

If there is one question that is most commonly-asked regarding the Ring o' Brodgar, and the neighbouring Standing Stones o' Stenness it has to be : "But what was it for?"

However, it's unlikely that the stone circles had a single purpose.

Just as churches today are used for various things weddings, burials, worship, meeting places, entertainment, etc it is likely that the stone circles served a number of roles.

Because of the effort involved in their construction, its fairly safe to say that they were important to the widespread community and, as such, these roles probably revolved around religion or ritual.

Theories abound some plausible, while others verge on the ridiculous.

Were they massive open-air temples? Communal meeting places perhaps? Or constructed purely as a means to map the heavens and measure the passing of time?

It could be all of these, or none. Despite the claims of many, we simply can't say for certain.

An astronomical observatory?

The results of excavations elsewhere in Britain, together with various finds at similar sites, do seem to point to a connection with the movement of the sun and the moon across the sky.

Astronomical alignments certainly seem exist at a large number of stone circles, perhaps even Brodgar, and this does add weight to the widespread theory that they were in someway used as astronomical observatories. Again, opinions on this topic vary, with as many detractors as supporters.

Professor Alexander Thom, an expert in the field of archeo-astronomy, spent several decades studying stone circles in an attempt to decipher their meaning. He discovered that not all were perfect circles some were egg-shaped others elliptical but whatever the shape they all seemed to show remarkable geometric precision long before the Age of Pythagoras.

Thom's conclusions were that the stone rings were definitely astronomical observatories.

At Brodgar, he felt the outlying mounds surrounding the ring were a key to this role going so far as to say that the mounds were more important than the standing stones themselves.

From the circle, Thom noted that the natural features in the surrounding landscape seemed to serve as distant markers for the rising and setting of the moon. A sightline to the cliffs of Hellia on Hoy, for example, seemed to mark the minor southern setting of the moon, while a notch on Mid Hill, to the south-east, defined the minor southern moonrise.

These facts, he said, proved that the ancient Orcadians used the monuments to gain a widespread body of knowledge of the moon's movements.

"The Brodgar site is the most perfect example of a megalithic lunar observatory that we have left in Britain.

The ring and ditch were probably placed on this little hill at first because from here there are four far-sights marking the approximate position of the rising/setting moon at the major and minor standstills.

Perhaps a thousand years later the accurate observatory was built from a cairn of earth, built with such accuracy that we can today date the observatory by the slowly changing obliquity of the ecliptic at about 1600BC.

Large mounds were built so that watchers could be placed on top to warn the people below of the impending rising of the moon."

However, Professor Thom was of the opinion that the Ring's 60 stones actually served the community as a sacred, or magical, ceremonial centre rather than being directly involved in the site's function as an observatory.

Although there may be an element of truth in Professor Thom's theories, it must be stressed that they are not universally accepted. His critics are keen to point out that the dates he puts forward for the construction of the ring, based on astronomical alignments, are around 1,000 years later than the accepted date of the ring's construction.

Ritual construction

In 2004, as part of the first in-depth study into the construction of Orkney's stone rings, archaeologist Dr Colin Richards suggested it was not necessarily the completed stone circles that were significant but rather the act of constructing them.

The prestige of erecting a fine megalith, he suggested, may have been the driving force behind the development of the monuments.

In his paper *Rethinking the great stone circles of northwest Britain,* Dr Richards, of Manchester University, challenged the long-held assumption that the monuments were intended to serve a purpose after their construction a purpose usually assumed to be of ceremonial or of ritual or religious significance.

Instead, he suggested that the act of building the monuments, in particular erecting the individual stones, was the ritually significant element and that the entire stone ring had no particular function. This, he suggests, may explain why there is a distinct lack of evidence that sites such as Brodgar were actually used.

Honouring the ancestors?

Or were the stone circles constructed to honour the ancestors? We know that the Neolithic people participated in some form of ancester veneration, but were the stone circles part of this?

One theory is that the Ring of Brodgar represented a symbolic area for the dead, while the Standing Stones of Stenness, with its central hearth, represented life.

The procession from Stenness to Brodgar, therefore, could be seen as a symbolic journey from life to death.

Others feel the stones themselves were erected to honour the ancestors, who, being a tangible link to the farming community's right to the land ratified their place within the islands' prehistoric society.

A prehistoric meeting place?

The sheer size of the Brodgar ring prompted the theory that it was designed to house the local population attending ceremonies or events.

According to Aubrey Burl, the Ring of Brodgar could have held 3,000 people. He went on to suggest that the Brodgar Ring was erected because the Standing Stones of Stenness grew too small to contain the increasing number of "participants".

We shall probably never know the real purpose of this enigmatic stone circle, and it's use, like our modern day churches and temples, was probably very complex.

Human burials, festivals of thanks, animal sacrifice, marriage, meeting areas or pathways to the gods all of these are possibilities. The only thing that is certain is that the Ring of Brodgar has captured the imagination of people for millennia and looks set to continue doing so for some time to come.

Temples of Sun and Moon

True tradition or romantic addition?

According to a number of antiquarian accounts, the Standing Stones of Stenness and the Ring of Brodgar went by their "traditional names" until the early 1840s.

The Ring of Brodgar was supposedly known as "the Temple o' the Sun", with the Stenness henge being "the Temple o' the Moon".

On first glance, these titles seem feasible enough, but are they actually authentic and not merely romantic additions of the antiquarians of the day?

I suspect the latter.

Given the persistence of placenames, and traditions, in Orkney, it seems particularly strange that these "temple" names if they were ever used to describe the rings completely disappeared from common use in such a comparatively short space of time.

Instead, I think they were simply erroneous terms applied by the antiquarians of the 18th or 19th centuries romantic additions, in the same vein as the infamous "Druid's Circle" and "Sacrificial Altar".

Lunar and solar links

One of the earliest accounts linking the stone circles with the sun and the moon was written, by the Reverend James Wallace, in 1684.

He states:

> "Several of the inhabitants have a tradition that the sun was worshipped in the larger, and the moon in the lesser circle."

But there is a danger of reading too much into this statement simply because we don't know who Wallace's "several inhabitants" were.

Had he referred to "peasantry" or "the vulgar" terms found in documents of the period to refer to "common" Orcadians then we could be more confident about the validity of the names. Instead, we are left wondering whether Wallace was actually misinformed by a well-meaning minister, or laird someone perhaps influenced by the ideas of "druidical circles" drifting up from the south.

It was around 96 years later that George Low, in his *A Tour through the Islands of Orkney and Schetland*, well and truly attached the title of "temple" to the stone circles.

In a passage detailing the Odin Oath, he states:

> "The parties agreed stole from the rest of their companions, and went to the Temple of the Moon, where the woman, in presence of the man, fell down on her knees and prayed the god Wodden."

He then adds:

"..after which they both went to the Temple of the Sun, where the man prayed in like manner before the woman.."

And that is more or less it when it comes to the documented evidence that the use of the names. Although Low's account bears the hallmarks of someone who has dealt with the common people, just how influenced was he by other accounts, in particular James Wallace's?

In 1851, the antiquarion F.W.L. Thomas had no doubts as to the celestial titles.

Referring to the Ring of Bookan, to the north-west of Brodgar, he wrote:

"..the Ring of Bukan, which was of course the Temple of the Stars, seems to have escaped notice, or we might have learned of some more ante-nuptial ceremonies performed there."

But just as we cannot say for certain that the titles Temple o' the Sun and Temple o' the Moon were traditional, neither can we completely dismiss them.

The possibility remains that the titles were the remnants of an ancient folk memory that may correspond to some of the current astro-archaeological theories regarding the original purpose of the stones.

But I doubt it very much.

The Standing Stones of Stenness

> *"Even in daylight the place has something uncanny about it. The Standing Stones of Stenness, mouldering, scarred and grey with age, rising as they do from an unbroken bed of heather always have a weird mysterious appearance."*

Standing at a maximum height of six metres (around 19 feet), the sheer scale of the megaliths that make up the Stones o' Stenness, make the monument visible for miles around.

Located by the south-eastern shore of the Loch of Stenness, only four of the ring's stones remain.

These are considerably larger than those found in the nearby Ring of Brodgar, approximately one mile to the north-west.

The Standing Stones of Stenness were originally laid out in an ellipse. Although it is commonly written that the monument was once made up of 12 megaliths, excavations in the 1970s suggest that the ring was never "completed", with at least one possibly two of the 12 stones were never erected.

Radiocarbon dates from the excavation show that the site dates from at least 3100BC, making the Standing Stones complex one of the earliest stone circles in Britain .

Like the Ring of Brodgar, the Stenness ring has been classed as a henge monument. The stone circle was surrounded by a rock-cut ditch (four metres across and 2.3 metres deep).

It was once believed that outside the ditch there was a substantial earth bank. This has been questioned in recent years an absence of evidence suggesting that there was no exterior bank.

With an approximate diameter of 44 metres (144 feet), the ditched enclosure had a single entrance causeway on the north side, facing the Neolithic Barnhouse settlementon the shore of the Harray loch. Little remains of ditch today, although traces remain visible around the stone circle.

Today, at the centre of the ring, the visitor will see a large stone hearth, similar to those found in Skara Brae and other Neolithic settlements.

The hearth was constructed from four large stone slabs, and, according to Dr Colin Richards, the excavator of the nearby Barnhouse Settlement, an earlier hearth was transplanted from Barnhouse to the centre of the stone ring.

Close to the hearth stand two angular slabs, standing side by side, with a large prone stone beside them. This is the remains of the "dolmen" rebuilt in 1907 although doubt remains that it was ever part of the original complex.

The Odin Stone and Watch Stone

Other megaliths in the vicinity, now thought to have been part of the original complex, are the Watchstone , a massive slab of stone that towers over the Brig o' Brodgar, and the Barnhouse Stone , a solitary stone to the south-east, between Maeshowe and the Standing Stones.

Until the beginning of the 19th century, the complex contained at least one other significant monolith the Odin Stone of Orkney legend.

Temple of the Moon?

An 18th century visitor to Orkney wrote that the Stones of Stenness were known locally as "The Temple of the Moon" a term he claimed remained in use until at least 1841.

However, the origin and validity of this term is questionable.

But temple or not, the ring was certainly involved in the later ceremonies and traditions surrounding the Odin Stone.

One historical account tells that during the five days of New Year feasting, lovers would visit the Standing Stones where the woman knelt and prayed "to the god Wodden" that they might keep the oaths they were about to swear.

They would then make their way to the Ring of Brodgar, where the kneeling "ritual" was repeated before finalising their pact before the Odin Stone .

Destruction at the Stones

n 1814, shortly after the Standing Stones were visited by Sir Walter Scott, disaster struck. A tenant farmer, tired of ploughing around the stones, began to demolish them.

After destroying the Odin Stone, the farmer, Captain W. Mackay, himself not a native Orcadian, turned his attentions to the Stones of Stenness. Before he was stopped, he had toppled one stone (Stone Five) and destroyed another (Stone Six).

The miscreant's actions raised such a public outcry that not only was legal action started, but attempts were made to burn down his house. The court action was dropped after Mackay promised to "desist from his operations".

In 1906, the Stones of Stenness were taken into state care and the toppled stone re-erected.

While this was being carried out, another, smaller, stone was found under the turf and raised using an existing socket-hole.

At the time, doubts were raised as to whether this small stone (pictured right, alongside the remains of the "dolmen") belonged in a circle that contained such huge megaliths:

'...within the circle was unearthed a large, ill-shaped stone, lying in a position, with its end in proximity to the next socket, as if it were the next monolith of the circle. Its shape and uncomeliness make one doubt what the position suggests'

'The ill-shaped stone ... with one end pointing to a socket, where no doubt an upright had at one time been, has been erected in the place indicated. Its end, we understand, suited the socket. We have doubts as to whether it is a genuine monolith. It looks such a dwarf amid these huge monoliths.... Mr Cursiter considers it is the broken part of the original stone, which is a likely explanation'

However, despite the protests, it remains possible that the stone's smaller size had some significance to the ring's builders particularly considering its position by the entrance causeway.

Sir Walter Scott's 'Sacrificial Altar'

In August 1814, the novelist Sir Walter Scott visited the Standing Stones of Stenness. There, he rather naively proclaimed that the central stone slab was: "probably once the altar on which human sacrifices were made"

Scott's description of the Stenness ring read:

"The most stately monument of this sort [circles of detached stones] in Scotland, and probably inferior to none in England, excepting Stonehenge, is formed by what are called the Standing Stones of Stenhouse, in the island of Pomona in the Orkneys, where it can scarcely be supposed that Druids ever penetrated.

At least, it is certain, that the common people now consider it as a Scandinavian monument; and, according to an ancient custom, a couple who are desirous to attach themselves by more than an ordinary vow of fidelity, join hands through the round hole which is in one of the stones. This they call the promise of Odin."

In 1907, Scott's "altar" was reconstructed to form just that a table-like dolmen structure in the centre of the stone circle (see pictures right).

This construction remained standing until September 1972, when the dolmen was toppled officially explained away as the result of a drunken prank.

Although the destruction of the altar is often blamed on a Hallowe'en prank, it is clear from a report in *The Orcadian* newspaper at the time that the altar was toppled some time before Hallowe'en:

Altar stone displaced for over a fortnight, people using the Brodgar road have noticed that the so-called "altar stone" at the Standing Stones of Stenness has been displaced and now lies on its edge against the supporting stones. Though spurious, it has become a familiar feature of the Orkney landscape. The police are making investigations."
The Orcadian. September 21, 1972

Local talk at the time, however, was that the dolmen had no place within the monument.

Discussions ensued as to whether the altar stone should be replaced, as there was actually no archaeological evidence that it belonged within the ring.

So, the archaeologists were called in and tasked to excavate around the base of the structure to find out, once and for all, whether there was any evidence of the "altar's" historical existence.

The excavations were inconclusive, but where the controversial "altar" had been raised, evidence was found that confirmed that some form of stone structure had indeed existed.

The form of this stone construction, however, was unclear, so it was agreed that the altar's two upright stones be re-erected and the "tabletop" slab left lying beside them.

And there they remain to this day.

> A Maeshowe connection?

Archaeological evidence seems to indicate that pairs of standing stones were once situated around the Stenness complex e.g. the Deepdale Stones, the Odin Stone and its companion, the Watch Stone and its twin.

The two stones, once thought to form part of the dolmen, were perhaps part of this symbolism.

It is intriguing, although perhaps mere coincidence, that the nearby chambered cairn of Maeshowe, when viewed from the centre of the Standing Stones (click here for a photograph) is aligned to the gap between the two "dolmen stones".

This could indicate that the stones formed some sort of symbolic link, or connecting "portal", between the tomb and the stone circle.

The Archaeological Excavations

The first archaeological examination of the Standing Stones of Stenness took place in the early 1970s.

Following the destruction of the central "dolmen", in 1972, a seven-week excavation took place over 1973 and 1974. This saw a series of trenches dug around the monument primarily to prove, or disprove, the dolmen's historical existence. Led by archaeologist Graham Ritchie, the excavations were enlightening to say the least.

They confirmed, for the first time, that the remaining stones had once been part of a ring containing at least eleven stones. Although a twelfth socket hole was located (No 12), it appeared to have been unused.

Geological examinations of the surviving stones revealed that five different types of stone were use a discovery that ties in with Dr Colin Richard's theory that the stones for the monument, just like Brodgar, were brought to the site from various different, perhaps significant, locations.

The excavators confirmed that the stone ring had been entirely surrounded by a ditch, apart from a single entrance causeway to the north. This stone-cut ditch surrounded an area 44 metres (144 ft) in diameter and was two metres (6.5 ft) deep.

During the excavation, the bottom of the ditch was found to be beneath the water table and therefore kept filling with water. This, together with archaeological evidence of aquatic plants, indicates that while the monument was "in use" the ditch contained water and, therefore, that water was a deliberate element of the design.

Inside the ditch were pottery sherds and the remains of cattle, sheep and dogs (or due to the size, perhaps wolves).

These could either indicate that offerings were thrown into it, or that the ditch was used to dump the refuse left over from the ceremonies inside the ring.

Bizarrely, two cremated bones from a human hand were also found in the ditch, near the entrance causeway.

The central fittings

At the centre of the ring was a large hearth, typical of those found within Neolithic dwellings, such as Barnhouse and Skara Brae.

Constructed from four large stone slabs, laid out flat to form a rectangle, the hearth contained traces of cremated bone, charcoal and broken pottery finds that strengthened the idea that the monument was once a site of feasting.

Later excavations at the nearby Barnhouse settlement, in the late 1980s, prompted Dr Colin Richards to suggest that an earlier Standing Stones hearth had originally been on the outskirts of the village, and relocated to the centre of the ring**.

The Stenness excavation showed that an upright post had stood in the centre of the ring prior to the relocation of the hearth.

Moving to the north of the hearth and running parallel to the entrance causeway, excavators found the sockets for a pair of standing stones. "Connected" to the hearth by a rough stone path, at some point the stones that stood in this position had been removed and the socket holes filled in.

Slightly to the north of these twin megaliths was evidence of a small, two-metre, wooden structure. Circular depressions at each corner indicated the position of probable corner posts. Tiny deposits of decomposed wood radio-carbon dated giving a date of around 2150BC.

The eastern and western sides of this feature were in line with the double megaliths, prompting the suggestion that the stone formed a "porch or monumental entrance" to the timber structure these stones may have been removed when the timber feature was dismantled.

In the place where the controversial altar had been raised, there was evidence that some form of stone structure had one stood on the site.

Although the stones that would be used to create the dolmen may have formed a stone setting parallel to the wooden structure and the paired megaliths directly to the south, the original stone-holes were destroyed during the 1907 reconstruction.

However, the excavators concluded that two eastern stone uprights were probably in their original position, with the socket hole for the third under the current "tabletop slab".

In this case, the stones continue the northward progression of features leading from the hearth a pair or standing stones, a stone feature and finishing with a parallel feature constructed with stones.

But because the exact nature of the "dolmen" structure was not clear, it was agreed that the two upright stones of the altar be re-erected and the "tabletop" slab left lying beside them. There they remain to this day.

Later use

South of the hearth-stones, a group of five pits were found, one of which was found to contain charcoal dating from between 469AD and 669AD.

This find may indicate that activity continued within the stone circle, perhaps even activity of a ritual nature, until well into the Iron Age and the middle of the first millennium AD.

The Odin Stone

Until the winter of 1814, a holed monolith stood in a field by the Standing Stones of Stenness.

This stone occupied a particularly special place in the customs, traditions and lore of the Orcadian people.

Thought to have been erected around 3000BC, the Odin Stone, or Stone o' Odin, stood approximately 2.5 metres (8 feet) high with a breadth of about one metre (3.5 feet).

The location of the Odin Stone was unclear until May 1988, when archaeologists, surveying over 8,000 metres of land surrounding the Stenness stones, uncovered socket holes for several stones and finally the socket of the Odin Stone itself.

The holed monolith was shown to have stood approximately 140 metres (150 yards) to the north of the Standing Stones of Stenness between the stone ring and the current house, aptly named Odin. A socket hole for a second megalith would indicate that the Odin Stone was once one of a pair.

But although the monolith had stood resolutely for millennia, the Odin Stone's destruction took less than a day.

Destruction

In 1814, the man who leased the land on which the stones stood an incomer by the name of Captain W. Mackay waged an attack on the Stenness megaliths.

At the time, the Odin Stone, and the circles of Stenness and Brodgar, still played a major part in common Orcadian tradition. Because of this, large number of people visited the ancient sites regularly. According to Mackay, this was ruining his land., so he set out to tear down the stones.

He began with the Odin Stone, which he destroyed in December, 1814, allegedly using the stone fragments to construct a byre.

This misguided "ferrylouper" the dialect word used to describe non-Orcadians living in the isles was already not well-liked, and his destruction of the monolith did nothing to improve this.

The native Orcadians were so infuriated by Mackay's actions that various attempts were made to burn down his house and holdings.

Then, on Christmas Day, 1814, a local historian in Kirkwall heard of Mackay's plans and involved the law who executed a "Sist and Suspension" against him.

By this time, however, Mackay had already toppled one of the Standing Stones of Stenness, and obliterated a second.

The monolith's fate

Though Orkney tradition maintained that the fragments of the Odin Stone were used for building material, in the 1950s, the local antiquarian, Ernest Marwick, could find no evidence to prove that this was actually the case.

He did, however, discover that the main portion of the stone the holed segment survived into the 1940s, before it too was completely destroyed.

This section of the stone, Marwick learned, had been used as an anchor for a horse-powered mill-shaft that moved around the parish of Stenness as the mill changed hands.

When it was finally decided to replace the horse-drawn mill with an engine-driven threshing machine, the old mill was uprooted and lay around, with the Odin Stone fragment, gathering moss.

Then, the day came that the owner's son decided to tidy up and remove the old machinery. Unable to move the stone segment, and ignorant of its history, he smashed it to dust.

His unwitting destruction of the Odin Stone fragment closed a chapter of Orkney history. But it also roused the fiery wrath of his father, who exclaimed:

> "You had no damned business to break that stone: that was the Stone o' Odin that came from Barnhouse!"

The Watchstone, Stenness

One of Orkney's most imposing monoliths, the Watchstone stands a short distance to the north-west of the Standing Stones of Stenness.

Towering over the Brig o' Brodgar, the solitary stone giant stands at the point the Stenness and Harray lochs meet.

Just over 5.6 metres high (around 19 feet), we know the Watchstone was once one of a pair of standing stones, outliers to the Stone of Stenness circle, that perhaps marked the approach to the to the Ness of Brodgar.

A second stone discovered

In 1930, the stump of the Watchstone's companion was unearthed in the bank by the side of the road.

The stump, which was removed at the time, was close to the edge of the Stenness loch, around 13 metres (42 feet) to the south-west of the Watchstone.

The stump measured 1.45 metres (4 ft 9 in) wide, 12.7cm (5in) thick, and at least 90cm (3ft) high.

It was aligned exactly north-east and south-west, at an obtuse angle to the Watchstone.

Its discovery led to the theory that the two stones were the remnants of the south-eastern section of a large stone circle, the rest of which has disappeared when the level of the Stenness Loch increased.

It has long been suggested that the two massive megaliths were once part of a stone-flanked ceremonial route between the Ring of Brodgar and the Standing Stones of Stenness complexes. Click here to view a map of the area.

Other megaliths said to have been part of this procession way included the Odin Stone, the Comet Stone, and two unnamed standing stones outside the house of Lochview.

However, a series of geophysics surveys carried out across the Ness of Brodgar have found no evidence of any stone avenue.

Another suggestion is that the twin stones may have represented a series of symbolic "doorways" between the two stone circles.

A midwinter connection?

Local man, Charles Tait, has highlighted an interesting connection to the Watchstone and the Midwinter solstice.

From the Watchstone, viewing the winter solstice sunset, the sun disappears behind Ward Hill on Hoy for a few minutes, before being "reborn" briefly at the bottom of the hill's northern slope.

A few days after the solstice, the sun sets behind Ward Hill, but this time reappears in a horizon "notch" formed by the island's hills.

This phenomenon prompted the idea that the stone was perhaps a marker for watching the sun's progress as it sets further and further south.

The various marker points afforded by the Hoy hills would allow the watcher to gauge the approach of the solstice.

The Yetnasteen, Rousay

The seven-foot high Yetnasteen stands at the foot of a hill in the north-east of Rousay, near the farm of Faraclett.

When the Norsemen arrived in the island, they had no doubt as to its origin.

The Yetnasteen takes its name from the Old Norse *Jotunna-steinn*, literally meaning *Giant Stone*.

This is a clear confirmation that the stone like a number of standing stones throughout Orkney was believed to be giant, turned to stone by the warm rays of the morning sun.

In Rousay, this petrified giant has one annual release from his eternal prison.

Immediately after midnight each New Year's Day, the Yetnasteen is said to come to life and walk the 300 yards to the Loch o' Skockness, where it drinks from the water before returning once more to its lonely vigil

The Stane o' Quoybune, Birsay

The Stane o' Quoybune, in Birsay, is a fine example of the many solitary standing stones that dot the Orcadian landscape.

Dating from the second millennium BC, and standing at a height of almost four metres (13 feet), the Stane o' Quoybune is one of a number of Orcadian standing stones attached to the folkloric motif of the "petrified giant".

Like the Yetnasteen, in Rousay, each New Year's Day, the Stane o' Quoybune is said to walk to the nearby Boardhouse Loch, where it dips its head to drink from the cold water.

Local custom dictates that anyone seeing the megalith on its annual trek will not live to see another New Year.

For this reason, on New Year's Eve, it was not considered safe to remain outdoors after midnight especially for those who intended to watch for the stone's movements.

The walking stone

Many stories circulated, most of which are now forgotten, of individuals who wished to see the walking stone for themselves. According to the tales, their corpses were invariably found the next morning.

One such story, documented in 1884, tells of a young man from Scotland who, upon visiting the islands, scoffed at the story of a walking stone.

Much to the horror of the locals, as the hour of midnight approached, the headstrong youth set out to begin his all-night vigil.

As time wore on, the foolish boy began to feel a growing terror gripping him, and an eerie feeling crept over his shivering limbs. At midnight, he discovered that in his frenzied pacing, he had wound up directly between the stone and the loch.

Turning to check on the monolith, he was sure he saw it move.

From that moment, he lost consciousness and his friends found him, at dawn, lying in a faint. When he regained his senses he:

"could not satisfy enquirers whether the stone had really moved and knocked him down."

Whether he survived to see the following New Year is not recorded, but it is doubtful that this young incomer would mock the islanders' beliefs again.

The rescued sailor

One of the more tragic tales surrounding the Stane o' Quoybune concerns a ship wrecked off the shores of Birsay.

On that cold, stormy December day all hands, save one, were lost victims of Teran's cruel reign.

The sole survivor found refuge at a cottage close to the stone, and, on hearing the tales of its annual march, resolved to see for himself whether such a superstitious yarn could be true.

In spite of the householder's protests, the sailor ventured forth on the last day of the year. To make sure he missed nothing, he clambered up on top of the massive megalith to await its stirring . . .

There he waited . . .

. . . and the first morning of the new year dawned over the body of the foolish sailor.

How he died remains unknown, but local stories recounted how the stone had rolled over the pathetic mortal as it made its way to the lochside.

The Barnhouse Stone, Stenness

The Barnhouse Stone is a solitary monolith, approximately half a mile (700m) to the south-east of the Stones of Stenness.

Standing in a field near Maeshowe, the Barnhouse Stone is clearly visible from the main Kirkwall to Stromness road.

On first glance, the lichen-covered stone looks fairly insignificant especially when compared to the Stenness giants a short distance away, to the north-west.

Appearances, however, can be deceptive.

The Barnhouse Stone is intriguing because it appears to be perfectly aligned to the entrance of the Maeshowe chambered cairn, approximately 700 metres to the north-east.

Local man Magnus Spence first recorded this alignment in 1893.

Then, in 1952, ex-provost Peter C. Flett OBE noted that:

"The alignment formed with this Barnhouse Stone and the long passasge of Maeshowe seemed to have peculiar significance, and was too remarkable to be merely accidental."

Mr Flett also suggested an alignment between the Barnhouse Stone, the Watchstoneand the Ring of Brodgar.

He remarked that the two standing stones formed a straight line with the centre of the Brodgar ring, in a north-easterly, south-westerly direction.

This line, he suggested, pointed to the position of the setting sun at Beltane May 1.

While the Beltane link is open to question, a definite alignment exists between the Barnhouse Stone and Maeshowe.

Standing just over three metres tall (10 ft), at the midwinter solstice, when the last rays of the setting sun shine through Maeshowe's entrance, the sun is directly over the top of the Barnhouse monolith.

The centre axis of Maeshowe's inner entrance passage is directly aligned with the centre of the Barnhouse Stone.

From Maeshowe, the line travels out to strike Hoy's Ward Hill at a place where the sun sets 22 days before and after the midwinter solstice.

This three-week period is referred to by archeoastronomers, such as Alexander Thom, as a megalithic month a sixteenth of a year.

Whether this alignment meant that the stone was put in place at the same time Maeshowe was built or was a later addition, erected to mark the alignment, is not clear.

The discovery of a socket hole to the rear of Maeshowe, that would once had housed another stone, seems to indicate that the Barnhouse Stone did have some function in the ritual use of the chambered cairn.

What makes this phenomenon interesting is the fact that if, as has been suggested, the Barnhouse Stone was an outlier to the Stenness ring and a part of the ceremonial complex, we have a definite link between the ceremonies held at the stone rings and in Maeshowe.

The Deepdale Stone, Stromness

Although Orkney is home to a number of well-known standing-stones, such as the Ring of Brodgar, it also has its fair share of lesser-known monoliths.

These stones, scattered across the islands, are often ignored because they are inaccessible, unnoticed, or, quite simply, don't look as impressive as their larger relatives.

The Deepdale Stone is a fine example of this.

Barely noticeable from the main Kirkwall to Stromness road unless you know when, and where, to look the Deepdale stone stands approximately two metres (7 feet) high.

Located on private ground, it pokes out from a crest of high ground on the western side of the current road, directly opposite the Stenness loch.

The Deepdale megalith once had a companion, but no visible trace of this stone survives today.

This second stone which, it is believed, was slightly taller than its companion was loosened after years of ploughing. It was removed sometime between the 1940s and the 1970s.

Subsequent excavation located the socket hole of the lost stone, along with its surviving stump.

The two standing stones' position, on the western horizon, led to the theory that the Deepdale stones may have been aligned, or were outliers, to the Ring of Brodgar, and connected to the setting sun in much the same way as the Barnhouse stone is to the chamber of Maeshowe.

However, the distance from Brodgar means that the Deepdale stones would have been very difficult to see with the naked eye.

As such it is hard to see how they could have been connected with whatever ceremonies took place within the stone circle.

Instead, the two megaliths may have had some connection with the nearby Unstan Cairn. The surviving stone looks down on the headland on which the cairn stands, its face turned towards the structure.

It is also possible that the Deepdale Stones were related to the nearby Neolithic site at Howe now destroyed. Again, however, this is debatable. In the Neolithic only one of the pair would have been visible, peeking over the crest of the hill facing Howe.

The Stan Stane, North Ronaldsay

At Holland, in North Ronaldsay, the most northerly of Orkney's islands, is a single megalith known locally as the "Stan Stane" a dialect term simply meaning "standing stone".

Over 13 feet high and three feet wide, the stone tapers from its base, narrowing slightly towards the top.

It has been suggested that this solitary monolith was once an outlier for a stone circle that may have stood around the Torness area of the island.

Like the famous Odin Stone, in the Mainland parish of Stenness, the North Ronaldsay standing stone is perforated the hole in this case about two metres up from the ground.

However, the hole in the Stan Stane is much smaller than that once found in the Odin Stone and there are no traditions of it being used in a similar fashion.

The stone is, however, the focal point for a centuries-old North Ronaldsay New Year custom that has seen the island's inhabitants gathering around it and singing.

Writing at the end of the 18th century, the Reverend William Clouston, minister of the Cross and Burness Parish of Sanday, said:

The Stone o' Setter, Eday

Perhaps one of Orkney's finest monoliths towers over a landscape dotted with chambered cairns, in the northern half of Eday

The Stone o' Setter is seven feet wide at the base and, at over 15 feet high (4.5 metres), is one of the tallest megaliths in Orkney.

Surrounded by ancient cairns, the Setter Stone stands in an area that was of some significance to the islanders of prehistoric times.

Centuries of weathering has given the sandstone monolith a distinctive profile. Tapering from the top, heavy erosion gives the monolith the appearance of a giant, stone hand a fact that has ensured it a place in local folklore.

But although the stone bears an uncanny resemblance to a giant's hand, tradition has it that it was raised by a local laird.

This laird first dug a massive hole to house his monolith, before piling up earth to form a slope by the hole. The stone was laid, on its side, on the ramp, with the intention of rocking it until the stone final slid into place.

However, despite the their efforts, the laird's men couldn't shift the stone. They just didn't have the strength to push the megalith upright. So, to help overbalance the see-sawing stone, the laird asked his wife to climb out and sit on the other end of the stone the end hanging over the deep pit.

The dutiful wife clambered out across the horizontal stone and, sure enough, it began to rock. As she jumped on one side, her husband and his entourage pushed the other, in an attempt to overbalance the massive, sandstone monolith.

As the rocking motion of the stone increased, the faster the wife jumped and the harder the laird's men pushed. Then, with a shriek, the laird's wife overbalanced and fell down into the socket hole. Seconds later, the stone crashed down on top of her.

According to the islanders, it was no secret that the laird detested his wife so made no attempt to remove her from underneath the Setter Stone.

Instead, the megalith was pushed upright and the hole filled with rocks and packed earth.

Burial Chambers and Cairns

Orkney's Chambered Cairns

Chambered cairns, or tombs, are the most common surviving constructions from Orkney's Neolithic past.

Found throughout the islands, usually visible as low, grassy mounds, these ancient constructions are generally thought to have served as burial places or, more correctly, repositories of the dead.

However, although the word "tomb" has long been used to describe these structures, it is perhaps a slightly misleading label and has lead to a widespread assumption that they only had a funerary purpose.

Just as today we would never think to refer to St Magnus Cathedral as a tomb although any excavator would find no shortage of human remains within its walls nor should we really label the chambered cairns of the Neolithic as such. Like the cathedral, through the ages, they were probably the focal point for a number of different social, practical or religious ceremonies.

The various theories as to the purpose of the chambered cairns are covered here.

The earliest Orcadian cairns were built by the first Neolithic settlers people who crossed the Pentland Firth from the Scottish mainland around the beginning of the fourth millennium BC.

The development of the chambered cairn in Orkney spans thousands of years, during which time a variety of different designs were adopted. Though these designs vary, they are now generally been classified as one of two main types the Orkney-Cromarty type and the Maeshowe-type.

These categorisations are slightly misleading, as Orkney's cairns do not necessarily fit into one category or the other. Instead we have variants of the Orkney-Cromarty cairns containing elements of the Maeshowe-type, while others, such as the Bookan cairn, don't fit in either.

However, as the terminology is fairly widespread, the two main classifications are:

Orkney-Cromarty cairns: These are typically made up of a single long chamber, divided into stall-like "compartments" by stone uprights. These cairns can also incorporate shelf-like structures at one, or both, ends. This style is not only found in Orkney but variants exist on the Scottish mainland. Although the Orkney-Cromarty tombs do not have side cells, a few hybrid chambers, such as Unstan in Stenness, have incorporated them in their designs.

Maeshowe-type Cairns: This style is unique to Orkney. The tombs have one main central chamber that is reached by a low, long entrance passage. One, or more, side chambers branch of from the main central chamber. Regarding the Maeshowe-style cairns, their construction, with larger, well-cut and fitted stones, is more monumental.

Dating from around 3600-3200 BC, the stalled structures represent the earliest phase of cairn development in Orkney and parallel the design of other early Neolithic buildings in the islands, most notably the house at the Knap o' Howar in Papay. They are also particularly associated with the Unstan Ware style of pottery shallow, round bottomed pots.

As time went on, the designs of the chambered cairns seem to have changed to mirror the evolving architecture of the domestic houses. Maeshowe, for example, representing the final phase of cairn development in Orkney, has a number of architectural similarities with the houses of Skara Brae in Sandwick. By the time of Maeshowe, Unstan Ware was no longer the predominant pottery style, and had been replaced by the more ornate, flat-bottomed pots known as Grooved Ware.

The continuous similarity between the domestic dwellings and the chambered cairns of the Neolithic has led to the idea that the cairns were regarded as "houses of the dead" physical dwelling places for the spirits of the dead, or the ancestors.

But it is important to stress that these "houses" were not mere crypts and played a significant role in Neolithic life.

From archaeological evidence, we can see that the early Orcadians went to incredible lengths to house the remains of their dead. The construction of a single cairn took considerable time and effort something that would imply that the dead or ancestors of each community were very important to their daily lives.

Whether we can class this reverence of the dead as a form of ancestor worship is unclear, but in a society where the average adult is thought to have lived to 30 or 40 years old, it is likely that offspring only knew their elders for a short time before they died. These people may therefore have considered the belief in some form of continuation after death important.

In his book, *Monuments of the British Neolithic*, archaeologist Miles Russell suggests that the use of the chambered cairns allowed the people in each area "stamp" their claim to the surrounding land. The cairns, holding the remains and therefore spirits of generations of ancestors, helped justify and strengthen a group's right to the land.

But human remains are not all that has been found within Orkney's chambered cairns.

The discovery of animal bones in some led to the suggestion that some form of animal totemism was practised. The discovery of sea-eagle remains at Isbister in South Ronaldsay and the dog skulls at Cuween in Firth has been at the forefront of this idea.

Maeshowe

"[Maeshowe is] one of the greatest architectural achievements of the prehistoric peoples of Scotland".

The parish of Stenness, in Orkney's West Mainland, is home to some of the county's best-known ancient monuments.

Among these is the prehistoric chambered cairn, Maeshowe.

Thought to date from around 2700BC, Maeshowe is one of the monuments that make up the Heart of Neolithic Orkney World Heritage Site.

Approximately 500 metres from the south-eastern shore of the Harray loch, Maeshowe is, by far, the largest and most impressive of Orkney's many chambered cairns.

Appearing as a large grassy mound, it is clearly visible for miles around, including the nearby Standing Stones of Stenness, the Barnhouse Settlement and the Watchstone.

Archaeologist James Farrer first excavated the cairn in 1861, prior to which the mound had a distinctly different shape than it has today.

As can be seen in the illustration (right), Maeshowe was once conical, with a deep depression in the top. It had a diameter of around 30m (100 ft) and stood 11m (36 ft) high.

The cairn was taken into state care in 1910, at which time a concrete roof was added to the structure. At the same time, the outer mound was sculpted to give it is present "rounded" dimensions of 7.3m high and a 37m diameter.

A Neolithic elite?

Maeshowe was built in the Neolithic period. Constructed on a platform of levelled ground, like the nearby stone circles of Brodgar and Stenness, the monument is surrounded by a ditch and raised bank.

Archaeological work in recent years hints that the cairn was built on top of an earlier structure perhaps an early Neolithic house.

It has been suggested that this house was replaced by a stone circle four of the stones of which came to be incorporated into Maeshowe.

An excavation outside the chamber, in 1996, led to the discovery of a socket-hole on a platform to the rear of the mound. This added weight to the theory that the site had one housed a stone circle.

The massive stone slabs used to line the entrance chamber may also have once been part of this stone ring.

At the same time, it was suggested that the chamber's encircling ditch was originally intended to be filled with water. This would have had the effect of further isolating the world of the living from that of the dead.

Maeshowe is made up of a large central chamber, with three side chambers built into the walls. It is accessed by a low, long entrance passage (see illustration below).

The complexity of the chamber's architecture, and the grandness of its scale, has led to the idea that Maeshowe was built to demonstrate the power of a "social elite" within the prehistoric tribal systems of the time.

Estimates for the labour required to build Maeshowe have been placed at 100,000 man-hours, compared to 10,000 hours required for its lesser contemporaries.

This, suggest some, shows a society where the emphasis had shifted from the community as a whole, to one elevated class, or individual.

The midwinter connection

Perhaps one of Maeshowe's most famous attributes is its midwinter alignment something it shares with the chambered tomb of Newgrange, in Ireland.

For a few days each year, as the midwinter sun slips below the horizon, its last rays shine directly through Maeshowe's entrance passage to illuminate the rear wall of the central chamber.

Stone ring links?

At the nearby Standing Stones of Stenness, stand two angular slabs, standing side by side, with a large prone stone beside them.

It is intriguing, although perhaps mere coincidence, that when viewed from the centre of the stone circle, Maeshowe is aligned to the gap between the two "dolmen stones".

This could indicate that the stones formed some sort of symbolic link, or connecting "portal", between the chambered cairn and the stone circle.

Viking invaders

During the 1861 excavation, Maeshowe's entrance passage was inaccessible, so an access shaft was driven down through the top of the mound. Once inside, however, the archaeologists discovered that they were not the first to break into the tomb.

Runic "graffiti" found on the inner walls confirmed the *Orkneyinga Saga* account that several groups of Norsemen had entered the tomb known to them as "Orkahaugr" in the middle of the 12th century and recorded their presence on the ancient stone.

The Isbister Cairn The Tomb of the Eagles
The discovery of the cairn

Like so many of Orkney's other prehistoric monuments, the discovery of the Isbister chambered cairn best known today as the Tomb of the Eagles was purely accidental.

The cairn was uncovered by a local farmer, Ronald Simison, on his land on the south-eastern tip of the island of South Ronaldsay in 1958.

After noticing flagstones jutting from a mound in a field, Mr Simison began digging and was astounded when, ten minutes later, he reached the bottom of what looked like a wall.

Excited by his discovery, he continued and, before long, had uncovered a black and white polished mace head, axe heads and a tiny jet button.

Spurred on by his unexpected discoveries, he dug further until he reached the top lintel of what he recognised as being an entrance of some sort.

Mr Simison continued exposing the newly discovered entrance bit by bit and was eventually able to peer into the darkness of the small stone cairn.

There, by the flickering light of a cigarette lighter, Ronald Simison saw the 30 human skulls that filled the chamber his first encounter with the long-dead occupants of the Tomb of the Eagles.

However, shortly after this discovery the tomb was sealed up again, pending a thorough archaeological excavation. But this promised excavation was a long time in coming.

More than 20 years passed years in which Mr Simison tried in vain to persuade the authorities to investigate the Isbister tomb. Eventually he gave up and decided to do the job himself.

The Bookan Chambered Cairn, Sandwick

The Bookan chambered cairn, to the north-west of the Ring of Brodgar, lies in what is arguably one of the richest archaeological landscapes in Orkney.

Today the cairn survives as a dilapidated oval mound, approximately 16 metres in diameter.

Inside, some of the internal chamber divisions remain visible.

Originally excavated in 1861, the cairn is close to the Ring of Bookan the ditch and bank "henge" monument at the northern end of the Ness of Brodgar.

The 19th century investigation revealed a rectangular central chamber surrounded by what appeared to be five smaller chambers.

Human remains were found in three of the side chambers, along with pottery and a flint 'lance-head'.

After the 1861 excavation, it was assumed that because of the structure's unfamiliar design, it had to be a very early example of a chambered tomb. It was, therefore, given a classification of its own and more or less forgotten about.

But the long-held assumption that the Bookan cairn dates from the early Neolithicappears to be contradicted by the pottery found by the antiquarian investigators.

The description they left has since been interpreted as being more like the later Grooved Ware rather than the Unstan Ware found in the early Neolithic period.

The fact that the site has similarities in both layout and architecture to Maeshowe and house two in Barnhouse has also muddied the waters considerably.

A two-week investigation in 2002 revealed much about the structure in particular that the antiquarians' early investigations had merely covered the earliest phase of its history.

Speaking at the time, archaeologist Nick Card explained: "After the original tomb, which measured approximately seven metres in diameter, had fallen into disrepair, it was incorporated into a larger cairn around 16 metres in diameter and bounded by three concentric stone revetments."

The 2002 excavations also highlighted a number of distinct differences between the Bookan and Orkney's other chambered cairns.

Nick Card said: "Various aspects of the tomb's layout, like the arrangement of the side compartments around a central chamber and the removable side-chamber 'doors', seem more akin to Orkney's

Maeshowe-type of tombs rather than the (earlier) stalled Orkney-Cromarty tombs, like Unstan."

But, he added, despite its similarities to Maeshowe, Bookan's size and architectural aspects remain noticeably different to other chambered cairns found so far in Orkney.

The Cuween Hill Cairn, Firth

The Cuween Hill cairn is built, unsurprisingly, into Cuween Hill, by the village of Finstown, in the Mainland parish of Firth.

The structure at the end of a trail that climbs up the east-facing slope of the hill.

Although small by Maeshowe's standards, the Cuween cairn is nonetheless an impressive feat of prehistoric engineering.

Cut into solid bedrock, the cairn comprises a main central chamber with four smaller chambers branching off from each wall.

Access to the interior is by a low, narrow, entrance passage, which, being less than one metre high, requires the visitor to get down on their hands and knees and crawl.

Once inside, however, the main chamber is fairly spacious and the visitor can stand comfortably although in pitch black darkness.

Today, the chamber is over two metres high, but the original roof which was damaged by 19th century "explorers" breaking into the cairn from above was probably higher.

Thought to date from around 3,000 BC, the cairn was excavated in 1901.

Back then, the remains mostly skulls of at least eight people were found inside. This small number led to the suggestion that, during its use, the chamber was cleared out periodically, with only the most recent, or significant, skulls left within.

The dog skulls

Aside from the human bones, perhaps the most interesting discovery was that of 24 dog skulls. This led to the suggestion that the tomb's users may have had totem animals.

However, over the years the relevance of these dog skulls has been queried, with suggestions that they may post-date the period the cairn was in use.

But recent radiocarbon dating of a fragment of bone, by the National Museums of Scotland, has confirmed the dog skulls and the tomb are contemporary.

So, just as the sea eagle was significant to the later users of the Isbister cairn in South Ronaldsay, perhaps the creators of the Cuween cairn venerated the dog, or held it as their tribal symbol?

One theory has it that dogs may have been used to strip the flesh from the dead before their remains were interred in the tomb.

Or perhaps the dog was seen as a guardian, watching over the house of the dead, just as they did with the nearby houses of the living.

Whatever the reason, all we can really say with any degree of certainty is that the dog was in some way significant to the people using the cairn.

Settlements

To the north-east of the cairn, on the side of Wideford Hill, is the Wideford cairn, while the site of the Stonehall settlement is in the valley directly below Cuween Hill.

Stonehall was an extensive Neolithic village that predates the Knap o' Howar in Papay.

Given the close proximity of the Cuween cairn to the Stonehall settlement, and the fact that the two were contemporary, would indicate that those who lived in the settlement were also responsible for the construction and use of the cairn.

The Dwarfie Stane, Hoy

The 5,000-year-old monument known as the Dwarfie Stane lies in a steep sided valley between Quoys and Rackwick on the island of Hoy.

A huge block of hollowed-out red sandstone measuring about 8.5 metres (28 feet) long, the Dwarfie Stane is thought to be Britain's only example of a rock-cut tomb. It should be stressed, however, that not all archaeologists share this opinion.

It is thought the chamber was carved out sometime between the Neolithic and the Early Bronze Age. Basing their dates on similar tombs found in the Mediterranean, archaeologists have settled on a date of around 3,000 BC.

Although it has been suggested that the rock fell, or was cut, from the rocky outcrop on the rock face above known as the Dwarfie Hammars this appears unlikely. The sheer height of the cliff face would surely have broken the rock in its descent.

The presence of another similar rock slab the Partick Stane about 200 yards along the valley would indicate that both stones were dropped by retreating glaciers at the end of the last Ice Age.

What makes the Dwarfie Stane remarkable is the fact that the massive stone was hollowed out using nothing but stone, or antler, tools, muscle power and patience.

An opening, three feet square, is cut into the middle of the stone's west face and leads into the inner chamber.

This chamber contains two rock-cut spaces resembling bed-places, both of which are too short for anyone of a normal stature. These were undoubtedly responsible for the origin of the dwarf folklore that surrounds the site.

The chamber's resemblance to a hermit's cell led to the stone being identified in the past as being the residence of a monk or hermit. At the time, proponents of this idea claimed that their theory was strengthened by the fact that visitors to the stone were in the habit of leaving offerings.

Lying outside the entrance is a large sandstone block (see picture right), which was originally used to seal the opening. We know that the tomb was still sealed in the 16th century.

At some point, it appears that someone attempted to break into the stone via the roof. This left a hole that remained until it was filled with concrete. There is no record of any archaeological excavation being carried out on the Stane, nor do we know what, if anything, was found inside.

A giant's residence?

According to an ancient Orcadian fable, the Dwarfie Stane was said to be the handiwork of a giant and his wife.

A third giant, who wanted to make himself the master of Hoy, imprisoned the gargantuan couple inside the stone. But his evil plans were thwarted, when the imprisoned giant gnawed his way out through the roof of the chamber.

This piece of folklore neatly explains the hole in the roof mentioned above.

Cave in the cliffs

In his memoirs, *Hoy, the Dark Enchanted Island*, Rackwick resident, John Bremner, documented the discovery of a cave high up in the cliff terrace behind the Dwarfie Stane.

During his exploration of the cave, Bremner came across an "egg-shaped" object that has been likened to some of the relics found in Skara Brae.

Could it be that the cave itself, although not necessarily the dwelling place of the workers, was somehow involved in the rituals surrounding the stone?

"The area round about the Stane is very bleak and rugged, the soil being boggy, and always wet, even in the dryest weather, providing no shelter of any kind. Also, the remoteness of the Stane from the nearest human abode even at that distant time lends to the belief that the prehistoric craftsman must have had his abode in close proximity to the scene of his labours, as to travel from either Hoy or Rackwick in bad weather, would, I think, be asking too much, even from our ancestors.

"The answer lay in the cliff terraces, and when home on holiday in the old place, I put my theory to the test; and I am glad to say that I succeeded in proving that such was the case. In these cliff 'terraces' there are a number of natural caves, and in the only one I entered for lack of time -1 found the floor was strewn with many layers of decayed heather; how many I had no means of discovering, nor had I any idea of at what depth the real bottom of the cave lay for I naturally concluded that there had to be a stone flooring at some depth.

"Among the debris on the 'carpet' of long decayed heather and grass, I found a beautiful egg-shaped stone, of hard-grained sandstone, and quite heavy for its size six inches long, with a circumference of five and a half. It was polished, and was, to my idea, a 'symbol' stone to the ancients the egg was the symbol of fertility."
John Bremner. Hoy the Dark Enchanted Isle

Although I have no doubt Bremner's cave exists, I have been unable to find it. I have searched the area fruitlessly. However, the one thing my searches of the area lead me to believe is that it is unlikely workmen scaled the sheer faces every morning and night.

It seems much more likely that they came from the region of the prehistoric settlement on the Whaness Burn, approximately one mile directly to the north of the Stane.

The Crantit Cairn, St Ola

The discovery of the cairn

Without a doubt, the most talked-about archaeological discovery of 1998 was the chambered cairn at Crantit, on the southern outskirts of Kirkwall.

Buried into a gently-sloping field, overlooking the valley between the beach at Scapa and the town of Kirkwall, the cairn had lain undisturbed for 5,000 years until one morning in April 1998.

On that day as had been the case every spring for countless years a ploughman entered, ready to begin work.

But there was one difference. On this occasion he decided to plough the field in a different direction to normal a seemingly insignificant decision that led to the discovery of what was hailed as one of "the greatest archaeological finds of recent years".

While ploughing, the tractor disturbed the roof of the tomb, dislodging a roofing slab. The slab fell to reveal a hole and daylight streamed into the underground chamber for the first time in millennia.

At first it was thought that the tractor had simply uncovered a burial kist a number of similar kists had been found in a neighbouring field in the early 1900s.

But closer investigation revealed otherwise.

Before long it was clear that yet another Orcadian chambered cairn had been unearthed. But this one was the first in recent years, and certainly the first that had not been disturbed since the day it was sealed.

The archaeologists were ecstatic. Despite the quantity of cairns scattered throughout Orkney, the new discovery raised hopes that the Crantit cairn would contain the undisturbed remains of early Orcadians.

Early hopes were for untainted DNA samples, skeletal remains and perhaps even fingerprints or footprints. So, with this in mind, the cairn was carefully sealed again to prevent contamination until a complete archaeological excavation could be made.

The Wideford Hill Cairn

Built into the north-western slope of Wideford Hill, a few miles from Kirkwall, is the Wideford Cairn. Around 328 feet above sea-level, this prehistoric structure is a Maeshowe-type cairn dating from around 3,000 BC.

Built on a steep hillside over looking the Bay o' Firth, the cairn's builders quarried into the slope to create a level platform on which to build their monument.

Unlike most other cairns in Orkney, Wideford's exterior stonework is visible today, lending the structure a "stepped" appearance, made up of three concentric rings. The cairn's earthen covering was removed after the monument was taken into state care, in the 1900s, but originally it probably looked like a domed mound within a retaining wall.

These days access to the chamber is through the roof, the original western entrance being 17.4 feet long and less than two feet high and wide.

Inside the cairn, three small side cells branch off from the main rectangular chamber, which is about five feet wide and ten feet long at floor level, but much narrower at head height. The side chambers are then built into the north, east and south walls.

During the 1849 excavation, no recognisable human remains were found, only a quantity of animal bones (cow, horse, boar, sheep and deer) among the rubble filling the main chamber.

There were no traces of pottery either, which, coupled with the absence of remains, seems to indicate that the cairn had fallen out of regular use before it was finally sealed.

The final ritual act surrounding the tomb was its deliberate filling with debris.

When the cairn was opened in 1849, the main chamber was found to be almost entirely full of rubble. The height of this rubble was above the level of the entrance passage which seemed to indicate that the material had been thrown into the chamber from the roof.

Closer investigation revealed a chimney-like structure that may have been built solely for this purpose.

Communing with the spirits of the dead?

A number of cairns in Ireland, and most recently the Crantit cairn in St Ola, have what are described as a "light slots" built into the structure.

Along with the theory that these slots allowed light to enter the chambers at specific times of the year, it has also been suggested that they may have been used for offerings of some sort.

Perhaps most interesting of all is the idea that the slots allowed the living, who undoubtedly participated in some form of ancestor worship, to converse with the spirits of the dead.

An intriguing theory is that the narrow slot could been used as some form of an oracle.

People might seek the advice of the ancients by asking their questions through the slot the echoes of their distorted words coming back as an answer could then be interpreted as they wished.

If this is the case, could the chimney-structure in the chamber roof, although definitely used to fill in the chamber at a later date, have had an earlier purpose?

The Quoyness Cairn, Sanday

The Quoyness chambered cairn, in Sanday, is yet another example of the Maeshowe-type cairns found in Orkney.

The Quoyness structure is located on the peninsula known as Elsness, in the Sanday parish of Cross.

In all probability, Elsness was once an island, perhaps separated from the rest of Sanday by a shallow stretch of water. Sand has now filled this in, to form what we refer to in Orkney as an "ayre".

The Quoyness cairn dates from the early third millennium BC (approximately 2,900 BC), and lies close to the shore, just above the high-water mark.

An arc of 11 Bronze Age mounds, connected by a bank, surrounds the Neolithic cairn. The presence of these funerary mounds, as well as the other 26 mounds that are scattered across the ness, seems to indicate that Elsness had some ritual, or sacred, significance to the Neolithic inhabitants of the area from the date of the cairn's construction through to the second millennium BC.

At the heart of the Quoyness cairn is the main chamber.

Standing approximately four metres high, this chamber is accessed by crawling through a nine metre long, low, entrance passage.

Rather than attempting to portray how the cairn originally looked, these days the external appearance of the cairn is meant to give the visitor an idea of the complexity of the various building phases Because of this, only half of the entrance passage is roofed.

A wide, stone platform surrounds the central cairn structure and, in all likelihood, when in use the cairn would have appeared as a large grassy mound, much like Maeshowe today.

Inside, six smaller chambers open off from the main chamber. Dug into the chamber's clay floor is a shallow pit and a short trench, both of which date from the tomb's original construction.

During exploratory work in the 19th century, bones from at least ten adults and five children were removed from the cairn.

Other finds included fragments of animal bone, pottery, bone and stone tools, along with two of the intriguing carved stone objects, similar to those found at the Neolithic village of Skara Brae in the Mainland parish of Sandwick.

The Unstan Cairn, Stenness

The Unstan, or Onston, cairn sits on a small grassy promontory jutting out into the salty water of the Stenness loch.

From cairn, the Ring of Brodgar and Salt Knowe are clearly visible, across the loch to the north-east, and the Deepdale monolith is silhouetted against the western horizon.

From the outside, the structure is not unlike a smaller version of Maeshowe a grassy mound. Inside, however, we find architecture distinct from Orkney's Maeshowe-type tombs, but sharing some elements.

The Unstan cairn is a classic example of the danger of categorising.

It fits neither in the Maeshowe-style of chambered tomb, or the Orkney-Cromarty design, but is instead a hybrid, incorporating elements of both styles.

Inside, large slabs of Orkney flagstone divide up the main chamber into stalls a feature typical of many of Orkney's stalled cairns. However, unlike most of these stalled cairns, which tend to be oblong or rectangular, Unstan is circular.

Not only does the circular shape echo the design of Maeshowe, but Unstan also has a side chamber typical of those found within the Maeshowe-type structures.

Because the roof of Unstan is modern, a concrete construction added after the site was taken into State care in 1934, a skylight gives the interior a bright and airy feel. A welcome change for those fed up of scrambling, torch in hand, around the inside of these Neolithic tombs.

The 7.8 metre (25.6 ft) entrance passage is low and narrow. Once inside, the visitor is faced with the side-cell opening, set in the wall directly opposite the entrance. During the 1884 excavations, two crouched skeletons were found within this cell.

The main chamber is 8.4 metres (27.6 ft) long and split into five sections by vertical flagstone slabs three central stalls and two shelved end-compartments.

Later burials?

When excavated, among the considerable amounts of bone found throughout, were several crouched skeletons.

As mentioned above, two of these were found in the side cell, the rest in the main compartment.

The crouched burials differ greatly from common Neolithic burial practice, in which the remains were brought into the tomb already stripped of flesh. The bones were not necessarily kept together but were mixed and rearranged among those of the tribe's ancestors.

As such, Unstan's crouched skeletons may represent burials made at a later period probably the last of the inhumations made in the tomb.

Unstan Ware

Along with the human and animal bones, an unusually large quantity of pottery was found scattered across the floor of the tomb. The fragments came from at least 30 Neolithic bowls, the distinct shape and decoration of which was identical to that found at the Knap o' Howar on Papay.

The sheer quantity of these Neolithic bowls found led to this specific style being named after the tomb. It is now known as Unstan Ware.

Unstan Ware was used at settlements such as the Knap o' Howar and was round-bottomed with linear decoration below the rim.

Carvings or 19th century graffiti?

Like Maeshowe, Unstan appears to have been visited at some time in the past by Norsemen. If they are not later "fakes" the carved twig runes can still just be seen on the stone that is now set above the entrance to the side cell.

Beside the faint runes is a deeply-cut carving of a bird, pictured above. Although a piece of carved grafitti identifies this as "Pictish marks" the age of the carving is not known.

The Blackhammer Cairn, Rousay

A short distance from Rousay's Taversoe Tuick, and built into a steep slope overlooking Wyre Sound, is the Blackhammer stalled cairn.

Thought to date from around 3,000 BC, the structure is a typical stalled cairn, with an interior divided into seven compartments by pairs of upright stone slabs.

Today, a modern roof covers the original remains of the cairn, which are are only a few feet high. Windows built into this concrete construction supply ample light to explore the site.

The original entrance was sealed up when the cairn was abandoned, so modern access to the interior is through a hatchway in the roof and ladder.

The structure is a 13-metre long oblong and was originally constructed with a distinct decorative design incorporated into its outer facing.

The stone slabs on the outside of the cairn were slanted to form a triangular pattern in the stonework. It is interesting to note the similarity between this pattern and the patterns scratched into the rims of Unstan ware pottery.

Traces of the decorative stonework can still be seen at either side of the entrance and when the entrance was finally sealed, the cairn's users went to great lengths to ensure the stones used were set flush to the wall and matched the pattern of slanting stones on either side.

The Blackhammer Cairn was excavated in 1936, with the remains of two men found inside. One body was in the most westerly compartment, the other lying in the entrance passage.

The fact that the cairn only contained the remains of two people seems to imply that the chambers were regularly cleared out the remains of the recently dead replacing those of previous generations.

Among the other finds were animal bones, stone and flint tools, the remains of an Unstan-style bowl and a burnt flint knife.

Among the other bones scattered throughout the cairn were those of sheep, ox, red deer, geese, red deer, gannets and cormorants. Many of these bones showed signs of burning or scorching.

Other finds included a section of an Unstan ware urn, a finely-made flint knife, two scrapers and five flint splinters.

The Taversoe Tuick, Rousay

The Taversoe Tuick or Taiverso Tooack, to give it its correct Orcadian name is a chambered cairn built into a sloping hillside on the south side of Rousay, overlooking Wyre Sound.

Dating from around 3000BC, what is particularly interesting about this Neolithic cairn is the fact that it is a two-storey structure, with one chamber set on top of the other. There is only other other cairn of this design found in Orkney Huntersquoy, on the island of Eday.

The discovery and excavation

The cairn was discovered in 1898, at which time it would have appeared as a small heathery knoll a perfect viewpoint for looking out across the Wyre Sound, towards Wyre, Gairsay and the Orkney Mainland.

This prompted the owner of Rousay's Trumland Estate, the infamous General Burroughs, to erect a sheltered seat where he might enjoy the spectacular views. It was during this construction operation that the cairn's upper chamber was exposed.

The discovery of the cairn, in particular the human remains within, disturbed Burrough's wife somewhat. She wrote:

"When I went to bed that night I could think of nothing else! There we had sat during many happy summers, stretched on the purple heather, basking in the sunshine; laughing and talking with the carelessness of youth, little dreaming that barely eight feet below us sat these grim and ghastly skeletons."

The two-storey site passed into the protection of the Ministry of Works in 1934, and, three years later, a thorough excavation took place.

The structure was found to have a diameter of about 9.2 metres. A platform made up of loose, flat stones surrounded the cairn with a clear, stone-free entrance leading up to the western side.

Two entrances were found one in the south-eastern side, leading to a lower chamber, with a second north-facing entrance passage leading to an upper chamber.

Although a gap in the upper chamber floor now allows visitors to access to the lower chamber by ladder, when the cairn was in use this was not possible each chamber was only accessible via its own entrance passage.

The outer chamber

Dug into the ground to the left, and slightly downhill, of the lower chamber entrance is a small chamber that has been described as a mini tomb.

This chamber is divided by four upright slabs and was found to contain three pottery bowls. No remains were found in the bowls but it seems likely that the outer chamber formed some part of the rituals that took place within the tomb.

The Knowes of Trotty

The Knowes of Trotty is one of the biggest Bronze Age cemeteries between Orkney and southern England.

Found at Huntiscarth, in the parish of Harray, at the foot of the western slope of the Ward o' Redland, the Knowes make up one of Orkney's earliest groups of Bronze Age barrows and were in use from approximately 2000BC-1600BC.

The site is made up of a series of 16 barrows earthen mounds, erected over individual burials arranged in two rows.

The mounds have suffered badly from erosion, caused not only by Orkney's notorious weather, but also local wildlife in particular rabbits.

The Knowes

Geophysics work in 2001 confirmed that the site once contained at least two more mounds, and, at one time, was probably made up of 20 barrows.

An excavation of the primary barrow, in 2005, revealed that it would once have appeared quite striking in the landscape.

The barrow was made up of a stone burial cist, flanked on both sides by two upright stones. It had then been surrounded by a stone "cairn", which was in turn covered in earth.

The barrow itself had been built into the top of a natural mound, possibly to enhance the visual effect, the base of which had been sculpted and revetted to suit the builders.

So, in its day, the barrow would have appeared as a conical mound on top of a stone-clad earthen platform.

The two "standing" stones inside the barrow are intriguing as there are, as yet, no parallels in Orkney's archaeology, and they don't appear to have been structurally necessary. Instead, they may have had some symbolic purpose.

The positioning of the twin stones bears a marked resemblance to the uprights found in Orkney's stalled burial cairns, although typical of the early Neolithic period, these predate the Trotty cemetery by centuries.

However, the Knowes of Trotty is one of the earliest groups of barrows in Orkney, and marks a transition from the burial practices of the Neolithic, when the dead were interred in mass communal tombs, to individual barrow burials and cremations.

But although funerary practice was changing, Bronze Age discoveries within chambered cairns in Orkney has shown that the structures retained some significance, were used, and may have still had a place in the rituals of the period.

Did the Knowes of Trotty stones represent some form of doorway a symbolic entrance to an "otherworld", or realm of the dead? Or were they dividing up the interior of the barrow in some way that was significant to the Bronze Age people who used the cemetery?

Lines of cremation pits were also found, dug into the saddle of the largest two mounds were also revealed. Characteristic of Middle to Late Bronze Age burials, these pits indicate that the cemetery was used for some time probably throughout the Bronze Age period.

Spectacular finds

Undoubtedly less well known than sites such asSkara Brae and Minehowe, the Knowes of Trotty are renowned for producing one of the most spectacular finds in Orkney's archaeological history.

In 1858, local antiquarian, and Orkney Sheriff Clerk, George Petrie reported the "excavation" of the largest of the barrows.

Within the earthen mound, a stone cist containing four exquisitely crafted gold "sun" discs was discovered, along with 27 amber beads and a number of burnt human bones. This find has, to date, been unparalleled anywhere else in Orkney.

The gold discs were made from paper-thin sheets of gold, decorated with concentric circles of zig-zags and lines. The largest of the undamaged discs had a diameter of 76mm and was holed in the middle.

They are thought to be covers for decorative "buttons", similar to those found in Wessex, in southern England. The style, however, is different enough to suggest that it was made by a craftsman attempting to copy the Wessex style. This appears to tie in with other Scottish Bronze Age finds suggesting that the Wessex style was prized by the elite and powerful people of the time.

Analysis also indicates the gold originally came from Scotland.

Wessex connections

The beads, like those unearthed in 1858, are of a style and design once found in Wessex, England. This would imply they were originally fashioned in prehistoric England, the necklace being brought to Orkney at some point in its life.

It seems likely that the necklace was old by the time it was place in the burial cist perhaps an heirloom that had been passed down through the generations. The age of the artefact is obvious from the wear on the surviving beads.

It is not clear, however, whether the necklace was complete when it was placed in the burial cist or whether it was deposited is broken fragments.

Whether the necklace, and the gold discs, were made in Wessex, or was manufactured closer to home, it is clear that Orkney had some connection to the people of southern England. This link between is further strengthened by the fact that the cemetery follows a design found around Stonehenge.

Dr Alison Sheridan of the National Museums of Scotland in Edinburgh has her own idea on this.

Speaking in July 2005, she suggests that at some point in the past, a group of Orcadians visited Wessex, where they picked up new ideas and fashions and took them back home. The Ring of Brodgar in Stenness, she suggests, could be an Orcadian attempt to recreate the massive stone circle of Avebury.

Who owned the grave goods?

We can only guess who was interred within the largest cist at the Knowes.

Given the nature of the artefacts buried beside them, the person was obviously of high status. But because the remains were cremated there's little else that can be said. It is not even clear whether the person was a man or a woman, although the necklace design, in a Wessex context, is usually associated with women. This would fit in with the decorative buttons, similar examples of which have been found associated with females in Wessex.

So do we have a matriarch or leader of a local tribe, interred with her most prized possessions or perhaps symbols of her rank in a cemetery that continued to be used for centuries after her demise?

On the strength of the surviving evidence we just can't say for sure.

A remote location?

One of the most common questions regarding the Knowes of Trotty are their apparent inaccessibility. Why build a grand cemetery in such a remote location? Visiting the site, the answer becomes clear.

The question itself is one related to our modern perception of accessibility. If we can't reach it quickly and by car, it's considered remote.

The Knowes of Trotty are situated in a regal position, with a vast swathe of the Orkney Mainland, stretching from the south-west to the north, visible under a dominant sky. What better place to situate the prominent grave of a high-powered, and wealthy, individual, and others from his community.

The site was long neglected, eclipsed by the gold treasures, which became its only claim to fame.

Thankfully, modern archaeological work has been redressing this and elevating the Knowes of Trotty to their rightful place in Orkney's ancient history.

Settlements and Dwellinghouses

The Stonehall Neolithic Settlement

One of Orkney's recent archaeological discoveries was the Neolithic village at Stonehall, in the Mainland parish of Firth.

The excavations at Stonehall were carried out over a three year period. During the 1999 excavations, I spoke with Dr Colin Richards of Glasgow University, the excavation director, to get some idea of what had been uncovered.

On the scale of Orcadian archaeology, what marked Stonehall as significant was the length of time the settlement appeared to have been in use. The excavation had uncovered a range of Neolithic houses which indicates a continuity of settlement throughout the Neolithic period.

The Kist House

Perhaps the most interesting discovery at Stonehall was a late Neolithic structure of a type never before encountered in Orkney.

Lying in the shadow of the Cuween chambered tomb, the structure a building with what appears to be a burial kist built into a raised floor was unlike anything Dr Richards had encountered before.

He explained: "First we thought it was a house but now it seems to have kists in it. So it's not a dwelling house. It's literally a building where there were burials of some sort."

The "kist house" was built in the absolute centre of the settlement and trenches opened around it clearly revealed the lower course of another late Neolithic house with its entrance facing the enigmatic building. With its hearth, stone furniture and bed, this dwelling would have been very similar to those now found at Skara Brae in Sandwick.

But one thing set the kist house apart from the surrounding houses the uncharacteristically shoddy workmanship.

Dr Richards explained: "It's not very well built and certainly wasn't as well built as a house. It's built on midden and they haven't bothered to put a decent clay foundation for the walls which they would normally do. So we can say it wasn't built as a dwelling."

When the kist was finally opened no remains, human or otherwise, were found and the excavation closed with Dr Richards admitting to being "quite puzzled" as to the structure's purpose.

An inversion of ideas?

"It must be to do with the dead because of the central kist. Having the kist where the hearth is in the other houses is, I think, really significant. When we think how important the fire was to the maintenance of life, they've substituted it for something to do with death. So it's a complete inversion." he said.

He added: "It may well be that it was somewhere where, when someone had died, the body was laid out, washed and dressed before being taken elsewhere."

As to the age of the mysterious structure, it was certainly from the Late Neolithic period, dating from around 3000 to 2500 BC but also contained another perplexing feature. A short distance from the kist and built into the floor was a bowl shaped depression formed of moulded clay. The purpose of this feature is not known but it may have had something to do with the activities carried out within the central structure.

Dr Richards went on: "The interesting thing is, we're constantly finding stuff that we do not understand. With a period like the Neolithic you get almost fooled into thinking we have some basic idea of what's going on, and then we look at something else and we're all at sea again."

"I think the reason for that is because to really understand something we have to make it familiar and if it's not familiar we simply do not understand it. All the time we're trying to make them like us but in reality these people were totally different."

The relationship to Cuween's cairn

What is particularly evident when visiting Stonehall is the site's position in relation to the nearby Cuween Cairn. Cut into the bedrock of the hill, the cairn is starkly silhouetted against the north-western horizon.

Whether this was deliberate is unclear but motioning over towards Wideford Hill, Dr Richards said: "The same goes for the other side of the valley over at Wideford. There's a settlement there in the same sort of position. From the location you see the Wideford Cairn silhouetted on the side of the hill. It's an interesting area and we're starting to understand how they were living in relation to the surrounding tombs."

The idea that the Neolithic chambered cairns acted as visible territorial markers for each individual community is a theory that Dr Richard thinks is far too simplistic.

"We've just assumed there's this one-to-one correlation, a bit like a graveyard with a township or village." he said.

"I think this is far more complicated and I wouldn't be surprised at all if there was this sort of general association between the tomb and the community but I think, given the materials we found in (the tombs) and the different architecture, that they could be related to different ancestors or different deities and so on. A far more complicated religious scheme than we give them credit for."

The Knap o' Howar, Papay

The island of Papay, lying about 20 miles to the north of Kirkwall, is home to 60 archaeological sites.

Among these are the incredibly well-preserved remains of the earliest known dwellings in Orkney — and the oldest standing buildings in northern Europe.

These structures, two oblong, stone-built houses, date from approximately 3,600 BC and were continuously occupied by a series of Neolithic farmers for at least five centuries.

The buildings, on the island's west coast, were uncovered in the 1930s when severe sea erosion revealed deposits of midden material, as well as evidence of well-built, stone walls.

This chance discovery led to the excavation of the site. After more than two metres of sand were removed, the underlying building was revealed. This "building" actually turned out to be two stone-built structures, placed side-by-side and linked by a passage through the joined walls.

At the time of the excavation, a few artefacts were uncovered but nothing that allowed the experts of the time to date the site correctly. As a result they declared the Knap o' Howar to be an Iron Age site.

More recent excavations, however, have shown that the Knap o' Howar was in use between about 3,600 BC and 3,100 BC. They were probably part of a small farm, the home of a Neolithic Orcadian family that remained in use for hundreds of years.

The two connected structures formed a dwelling house and a multipurpose workshop/barn. With walls still standing to a height of 1.6 metres (5 feet), the dwellinghouse is the largest and best preserved of the two buildings. It is reasonably spacious and divided into two living areas by large upright stone slabs.

The outer chamber has a low stone bench running along the wall, while excavations in the other chamber indicated that it was probably a kitchen of sorts, with a central hearth and footings for wooden benches.

The large stone quern, used for grinding barley, together with a smaller variant still lie where they were found all those years ago.

The "workshop" has a similar entrance to the main house but was separated inside into three distinct areas by a series of large stone slabs.

A few curious facts surround this section of the structure such as the fact that the door joining the two sections was set in the workshop side. From this, it would appear that the workshop went out of use during the life of the main house, for both its entrances were found to have been blocked with stones.

The excavations also revealed that the current houses were not the first on the site, but may actually have been built upon the midden remains of an earlier, even older, structure.

Skara Brae

The discovery of the village

"On the far curving shore of the bay lies Skara Brae, hazy through the sea-haar."
George Mackay Brown *Rockpools and Daffodils*

On the southern shore of the Bay o' Skaill, in the West Mainland parish of Sandwick, is the Neolithic village of Skara Brae one of Orkney's most-visited ancient sites and regarded by many as one of the most remarkable prehistoric monuments in Europe.

In the winter of 1850, a great storm battered Orkney.

There was nothing particularly unusual about that, but, on this occasion, the combination of wind and extremely high tides stripped the grass from a large mound, then known as "Skerrabra".

This revealed the outline of a number of stone buildings something that intrigued the local laird, William Watt, of Skaill, who embarked on an excavation of the site.

In 1868, after the remains of four ancient houses had been unearthed, work at Skerrabra was abandoned. The settlement remained undisturbed until 1925, when another storm damaged some of the previously excavated structures.

A sea-wall was built to preserve these remains, but during the construction work, yet more ancient buildings were discovered.

"I hear, says the writer in The Bulletin, that the excavations at Skerrabrae in Orkney, which attracted so much attention last year, are to be resumed at an early date.

"Professor V. Gordon Childe will again co-operate with the representatives of the Office of Works.

"There are still some problems to be solved, and its hoped that this

season's researches will throw a flood of light on the period of the underground structures and the people who dwelt in them."
The Orcadian, July 4, 1929

'Modern' investigations

Further excavations followed and, between 1928 and 1930, the dwellings we see today were released from their protective cocoons.

At the time, the village was thought to be an Iron Age settlement, dating from around 500BC but this was no Pictish village.

Radiocarbon dating in the early 1970s confirmed that the settlement dated from the late Neolithic inhabited for around 600 years, between 3200BC and 2200BC.

Today, Skerrabra or Skara Brae as it has become known survives as eight dwellings, linked together by a series of low, covered passages.

Because of the protection offered by the sand that covered the settlement for 4,000 years, the buildings, and their contents, are incredibly well-preserved.

Not only are the walls of the structures still standing, and alleyways roofed with their original stone slabs, but the interior fittings of each house give an unparalleled glimpse of life as it was in Neolithic Orkney.

Each house shares the same basic design a large square room, with a central fireplace, a bed on either side and a shelved dresser on the wall opposite the doorway.

In its lifetime, Skara Brae became embedded in its own rubbish and this, together with the encroaching sand dunes, meant the village was gradually abandoned.

Thereafter, the settlement was gradually covered by a drifting wall of sand that hid it from sight for for over 40 centuries.

But the elements that exposed Skara Brae to the world are also its greatest nemesis.

The village remains under constant threat by coastal erosion and the onslaught of the sand and sea. In addition, the increasing number of visitors to the site annually are causing problems. Steps are being taken, however, to alleviate, or minimise, this damage.

The Barnhouse Neolithic Settlement

By the south shore of the Harray loch, on a point of land called Antaness, around 150 metres to the north of the Standing Stones o' Stenness, are the remains of an Orcadian Stone Age settlement.

Now known simply as the Barnhouse Settlement, only the reconstructed lower courses of a small section of the village's stonework are visible today.

But although these meagre remains are nowhere near as impressive as its contemporary, Skara Brae, the Barnhouse Settlement is particularly interesting for a number of other reasons.

Barnhouse revealed

The village was discovered in the winter of 1984, after a field-walking exercise undertaken by archaeologist, Colin Richards.

Agricultural activity over the centuries meant that little remained of the site, but the resulting excavations uncovered evidence of 15 small dwellings in varying stages of development.

The structures were round perhaps with timber and turf roofs with turf cladding surrounding the outer walls. Because there were no roofed passageways between the huts such as those at Skara Brae it appears that the Barnhouse dwellings were free standing and not encased in midden.

But particularly intriguing was the fact that each building appeared to have been deliberately demolished at the end of its life.

Today, although only the reconstructed lower walls are visible, the similarities between Barnhouse and Skara Brae are obvious. This is not particularly surprising given the two villages were in use at the same time. On closer examination, however, it becomes clear that the Barnhouse structures actually differ in style to Skara Brae.

This difference, however, is not great and probably due to the fact that the Barnhouse settlement fell out of use 450 years before Skara Brae. As such, its architecture did not develop to the same extent.

Indeed, excavation at Skara Brae has shown that its earliest dwellings were relatively similar to the Barnhouse structures.

Elaborate structures

But despite the architectural differences, the Barnhouse Settlement visitor will still be able to pick out the similarities between the two ancient settlements both have the same central, kerbed hearths, recessed box-beds and stone furniture.

But two of the Barnhouse buildings are very different.

These structures House Two and Structure Eight are larger and more elaborate than the other buildings at Barnhouse or Skara Brae.

These differences, clearly apparent on the site plan to the right, prompted the theory that the structures were built to house someone of importance within a tribal hierarchy.

We know the Barnhouse settlement was in use at the same time as the Standing Stones o' Stenness and within the largest structure is a central hearth, similar to the one in the Stenness henge.

Was the settlement created to house certain individuals who were instrumental in the construction of the stone ring? This might explain why the buildings were demolished after use when the project was completed the artisans moved on.

Home of a priesthood?

Another idea is that the village was constructed to house an elite class of "priest".

This theory originally surfaced a number of years before Barnhouse was discovered, when it was suggested that Skara Brae was the home of "priests" who officiated at tribal ceremonies in and around the Stenness rings. At the time, however, the idea was abandoned, only to be resurrected after the Barnhouse settlement was found.

The design of House Two seems to fit with this idea as there are structural similarities between it and Orkney's chambered cairns.

Perhaps this building was not a mere dwelling but was actually some form of meeting hall, connected with the ceremonies at the nearby stone rings. Or were the tribal wise-men cloistered in this sacred compound, close to their ceremonial centre?

The ritualistic elements apparent in the design of the Barnhouse settlement and its location in the ceremonial heartland of Neolithic Orkney the Ring o' Brodgar, the Stenness Stones and Maeshowe are all clearly visible from Barnhouse certainly lends weight to this idea.

A clear connection between Barnhouse and the Standing Stones o' Stenness is the large stone hearth found in the centre of the stone circle. This hearth was constructed from four large stone slabs, and, according to Colin Richards, was transplanted Barnhouse to the interior of the ring.

The Ring of Bookan, Sandwick

About a mile to the north-west of the Ring of Brodgar, is the site of what appears to be another prehistoric henge the Ring of Bookan.

This massive earthwork comprises an enclosing ditch surrounding an oval raised platform, measuring about 44.5 metres by 38 metres.

The interpretation of the Ring of Bookan is not clear, although a recurring suggestion in the past was that it housed a Maeshowe-type cairn. Other suggestions are that the enclosed platform once featured a series of standing stones, or a cairn.

The dimensions of the Bookan "ring", however, hint at a connection with the nearby Standing Stones of Stenness.

At two metres deep and 13 metres across, the Bookan ditch is wider than the ditches found at both Brodgar and the Standing Stones, but similar in depth to the Stenness henge. The enclosed area of the Ring of Bookan is also almost identical to that of the Stones of Stenness.

The Bookan henge lacks two features common to Brodgar and Stenness an entrance causeway and outer bank. These, however, could easily have fallen victim to ploughing and farming over the centuries.

Within the ditch are a number of stones and a rough mound. It has been suggested that this is the remains of a cairn, but this remains speculation

Iron Age Orkney

Minehowe The Underground Enigma

A mystery reopened

In 1999, there was one archaeological site that turned all eyes to Orkney Minehowe, a mysterious, underground structure, buried deep within a mound in Tankerness.

Within days of the howe being reopened, by landowner, Douglas Paterson, the tale of the two-storey construction had made it to the national, and international, press albeit with some fairly sensational additions.

One such account hailed the chamber as a "druid's temple", while others went as far as to manufacture "an aura of evil" that, they claimed, had caused the site's original excavators "to flee in such terrified haste that they were forced to leave their tools behind".

But there was one crucial point that practically all the reports got wrong.

Minehowe was not a new discovery.

The chamber was first opened in 1946, and was undoubtedly known about for some time before that. But this, and the fact that many folk in Tankerness were well aware of its existence, did nothing to dim the media attention.

What is Minehowe?

Dating from the Iron Age, Minehowe is an underground, stone-built chamber, dug into a large, earthen mound.

Access to the chamber is by a steep, ladder-like, staircase of narrow stone steps. The first flight of steps takes the visitor down to a narrow landing, from which two long, low chambers branch out at almost right angles.

From here, like a spiral staircase, a second steep flight of steps leads down into the darkness until it reaches a sudden drop of about five feet into the lower chamber at the bottom of the structure.

Approximately 20 feet from the top of the howe, this small chamber was thought to be a well by the 1946 excavators, who recorded that it had contained bones and ashes. But when it comes to the exact purpose of the structure, modern archaeologists remain puzzled.

Although the experts who studied the chamber in 1946 emphatically labelled it a broch, we can now rule out that theory. When it comes to the role of Minehowe, it is generally agreed that the structure has a ritual or religious purpose perhaps a symbolic entry to the underworld, or a place to commune with the spirits of the earth.

Within the lower of the two "first floor" chambers was a broken hammer stone. Alongside was the skull of a small dog a find that echoes the discovery of 24 dog skulls at the Cuween chambered cairn, outside Finstown. Was this skull left here for a reason? Perhaps guarding, or protecting, the entrance. The discovery added weight to idea that the structure had a ritual purpose.

Minehowe is surrounded by a massive ditch, similar to that surrounding the Ring o' Brodgar in Stenness. The could imply that the enclosed are had been considered in some way special the ditch perhaps marking a boundary between the sacred and common ground.

"The Orkney Mystery of the 29 Steps"

Aside from a second, intact, hammer stone, and the tools abandoned by the excavators, nothing else was left on site after the 1946 excavation work.

Back then, *The Orcadian* newspaper, of August 29, 1946, christened the discovery "the mystery of the 29 steps" and told how the jubilant diggers brought back to the surface "stone axes, knives, hammers and a piece of clay urn."

As well as the "hundreds of bones and other relics were strewn about the floor of this chamber", the report goes on to explain that also among the items found were "curious polished stones (fairly common in Orkney excavation), two teeth and some bones".

Another hole revealed quantities of cockle shells, a find which convinced the excavators that they had to be working on an ancient dwelling.

Orkney's Underground 'Earth-houses'

A prehistoric enigma

An enigmatic type of prehistoric structure found in Orkney goes by the uninspiring title of "earth-house". Dating from the late Bronze and and early Iron Age, these earth-houses generally known as souterrains elsewhere in Britain usually comprise of a long, underground entrance passage leading to a round chamber.

Some British souterrains are visible above ground, but the Orcadian versions are completely subterranean. Sometimes, as in the case of the Grain earth-house, the chambers were built quite deep underground.

These chambers, of which two fine Orcadian examples remain open to the public, date from sometime in the first millennium BC. Why they were built, and what they were used for, however, remains a topic of debate. The discovery of the remains of 18 people in the Rennibister earth house in Firth really muddied the waters in this respect.

Until recently, there was little modern excavation work concentrating on Orkney's earth houses, but their association with domestic structures, i.e. houses, led to the assumption they too had a purely domestic function usually storage.

But there are problems with this interpretation.

Firstly, there is a distinct lack of evidence to show what, if anything, was ever stored in the chambers. Secondly, as any modern visitor will attest, there are obvious difficulties involved in accessing the underground chamber.

Recent excavations however, would indicate the earth-houses were not mere storerooms but had a more ritualistic, or religious, purpose.

After three years work on an earth-house at Windwick, in South Ronaldsay, it would appear that earth-houses had as much to do with ritual, and in particular the dead, than a place to stash that season's crops

Orkney's Brochs

The massive Iron Age structures known as brochs are unique to north and west of Scotland.

Huge, drystone towers, brochs are concentrated mainly in the northern tip of the Scottish mainland and the Northern Isles, with some also scattered across the west coast of Scotland and the Western Isles.

In total, at least 700 brochs are known to have existed across Scotland, constructed and developed over the period between 600BC and 100 AD. Of these, archaeologists know of at least 50 in Orkney.

The actual number of Orcadian broch sites is likely to be much higher, however, as there are numerous unexcavated mounds throughout Orkney that probably contain broch remains.

What is a broch?

A typical broch stood from five to 13 metres high. It was a circular, two-storey, drystone, structure, accessed by a single door at ground level.

Inside was a main inner "chamber" from which smaller cells either built into, or up against, the wall branched off. A winding, stone staircase, housed within the broch's double walls, led upwards to elevated floors and finally the top of the structure.

Although, like the earlier roundhouses, it is possible that some brochs were no more than fortified dwellings, a widespread belief is that they had a defensive function and are characterised by immensely thick outer walls.

It is now believed, however, that, although defence may have played some part, they were more likely to have been built to impress a monumental marker in the landscape, highlighting the owner's social status, wealth and power.

Orkney's brochs were feats of considerable architectural and engineering expertise, the key to which was the principle of double-skinned walls.

Stronger and more stable than a single wall, the brochs had two parallel walls built with a hollow space between. These two outer "skins" were bonded at certain heights by stone lintel slabs a method that allowed the broch's constructors to build to greater heights than could be achieved with solid walls.

"To construct stable walls of such height, in unmortared masonry or undressed stones shaped only by splitting, called for an engineer's understanding of force and stress."
Dr Raymond Lamb

Underground chambers

An intriguing element about the construction of Orkney's brochs, is that many of them were found to have an underground chamber, often accessed via a flight of stone steps.

At one time, these chambers were dismissed as domestic wells, or cellars, but recent research has hinted at a more ritual use.

Holy Sites

Eynhallow The Holy Isle

The 'lost' kirk
The island of Eynhallow lies between the Orkney Mainland and Rousay.

Abandoned in 1851, the 75-hectare island is surrounded by ferocious tidal races known in Orkney dialect as "roosts. These roosts are at their most spectacular when the wind is in the north-west and a strong tide is running.

Now uninhabited, Eynhallow the Norsemen's *Eyin Helga*, Holy Island has a special place in Orkney tradition and folklore.

Originally believed to be the summer home of theFinfolk, the island was wrested from them by the guile of an Orkney farmer.

At its centre, stands the ruins of a chapel, which may have formed part of an early Christian monastic settlement. But although we now know of its ecclessiastical origins, it was not always so.

Standing by the skeletal remains of two old houses, it is immediately clear why the original purpose of the Eynhallow kirk remained unknown for over 400 years. It is, quite simply, decidedly un-churchlike.

Although the structure not only served the spiritual needs of the island's early population, from the 16th century, it was used as a dwelling by a number of the islanders.

Their later structural additions a complex of thatched roof cottages served to mask the building's original role, until, in 1851, disease and death among the four families who lived there led to the evacuation of the island.

The site was abandoned, and Eynhallow left to seabird and seal.

This disease is traditionally said to have been typhoid, ascribed to the well, Kairikelda, which it is claimed, lay below a midden which polluted the water supply. How much truth is in this remains unknown.

Following the outbreak, and to make the buildings uninhabitable, the roofs were torn off. It was only then that it became clear that an ancient church lay at the core of the complex.

From the outside, the modern visitor would still be hard-pressed to guess at the original function, but once inside, the sight of two ornate stone arches makes it immediately apparent.

Built to a Romanesque design, the church has a rectangular nave, opening at the east end into a rectangular chancel. At the west end was a substantial square porch which, it has been suggested, could actually be the remnants of the lower walls of a square church tower. Narrow doorways allow access to the interior.

An intriguing mystery surrounds a number of red sandstone fragments that lie in one of the kirk's outbuildings. It is thought these stones were found during the 19th century clearance of the site, but their purpose remains unknown.

They do, however, have a distinct resemblance to the stonework found in the St Magnus Cathedral in Kirkwall.

The Eynhallow Kirk is made from local stone, so the red sandstone, as used in the cathedral, must have been imported for a reason.

Years ago, Dr Raymond Lamb, then the Orkney archaeologist, suggested that construction on the church began around 1150, following the style of St Magnus Cathedral. Were these "soft" sandstone fragments originally incorporated into the interior design of the Eynhallow kirk, but later removed when it became a domestic settlement?

As Dr Lamb concluded: "The fragments on Eynhallow, however, remain an enigma."

But what about the monastery?

The Brough of Deerness

Jutting out into the North Sea, on the north-eastern coast of the Orkney Mainland, is a large grassy rock known as the Brough of Deerness.

Measuring 80 metres wide, and surrounded by 30 metres sheer cliff faces, on top of the Brough are faint traces of a settlement, surrounding the visible remains of a 10th century chapel.

The site was once connected to the Orkney Mainland by a land bridge, but a geologist's examination in 2008, confirmed this had crumbled away a long time before it was occupied.

Now the site is not one of the easiest to reach the visitor must first negotiate a slippery and muddy descent to the bottom of Little Burrageo, before a steep, narrow ascent along the south face of the Brough to reach the summit.

Once on the Brough, the visitor will immediately spot the remains of the chapel, which stand four of five feet high. Dating from the late

Norse period, this chapel is the focus of a complex archaeological mosaic, consisting of a bank and wall and a tight cluster of an estimated 30 structures.

Because of the account of the Brough by Jo Ben, allegedly dating from 1529, it had been known for some time that the land bridge must have collapsed before the 16th century.

Jo Ben wrote:

"In the north part of the parish there is, in the sea, a natural rock where the people on hands and knees ascend to the top with great difficulty."

In addition, the site is referred to as the "Borch of Dernes" in a 14th century list of islands in Orkney, compiled by John de Fordun.

However, during long-awaited excavation of the site in 2008, an examination of the area highlighted a geological fault a fault, which saw the land bridge collapse a long time before the Brough settlement.

The project's geologist, Professor Donna Surge, was clear: "There could not have been a land bridge there 1,000 years ago."

Instead, she suggested a bridge had been constructed to provide access. And that at the Brough-side of this bridge, which would have been no mean feat of engineering, was a defensive rampart.

This defensive structure, with masonry showing on the landward face, is still clearly visible and has led to much speculation over the years.

Some suggested it represented Iron Age earthworks while others declared them to be a "Vallum Monasterii" a symbolic barrier for the theoretical monastery.

However, the 2008 excavation director, Dr James Barrett, from the University of Cambridge, felt that, based on the current evidence, the bank and wall was a Norse construction, although possibly reusing an existing feature, was defensive and controlled access to the site another outwardly visible show of power, prestige and wealth.

Despite excavations on the Brough in the 1970s, until 2008, nothing was known about the site to allow it to be dated exactly, or even show what it was used for. But a five-week excavation, by the University of Cambridge, remedied this.

From the late 19th century, the idea that the Brough was an early, pre-Norse, "ecclesiastic settlement" became common. This theory was first aired in 1879, and subsequently gained antiquarian popularity. More recently, however, scholars firmly placed the rectangular buildings in the Viking era, dating from the 11th and 12th centuries.

From work so far, Dr Barrett feels the Brough was the site of a Viking chieftain's settlement a fortified stronghold that was also a visible show of power and prestige.

"In the past it's sometimes been a matter of academic fashion as to whether it was declared monastic or a defended site. At the moment I'm leaning toward this site as being a chiefly settlement, rather than a monastic enclosure," he said.

"Chris Morris, who excavated the chapel in the 1970s, first raised the idea that the Brough was a chieftain's stronghold, and the new evidence is pointing in that direction. If, for the sake of argument, we say it was a chiefly site, then why here? It's very strange. At the end of the day, I think it comes down to somebody making a point."

The 2008 excavations uncovered the remains of two Norse houses. Although full examination of the artefacts found inside will be required to provide a precise date, Dr Barrett suspects the structures date from the 11th century and are, therefore, contemporary with the last phase of the nearby chapel.

"Although we'll never be able to directly link the settlement, stratigraphically, to the chapel, there were a number of burials found during the excavation of the chapel in the 1970s. One of these was buried against the chapel wall, and was radio-carbon dated to the 11th/12th century. From this, we can see that the chapel is contemporary with the later settlement structures."

The architecture of these Norse houses is particularly intriguing. They follow a plan commonly found in Viking-Age Dublin making the cluster of houses reminiscent of an urban housing site in a rural location.

Although the buildings were built into earlier structures, it's not yet clear what these are whether Norse or earlier.

That the excavated later structures were domestic is without question finds included loom weights, soapstone pot, pottery and a spindle-whorl but there also appeared to have been metalworking carried out on site. Used mould sections were found, but these were too fragmented to allow the archaeologists to ascertain what they were used for.

St Magnus Kirk, Egilsay

The roofless remains of St Magnus Kirk stand on the western side of Egilsay dominating the island on which St Magnus was executed early in the 12th century.

Built towards the end of the 12th century, the church is made up of a rectangular nave and a square chancel, with a tall round tower on the western end. Despite the lack of a roof, the remains are still in good condition.

The tower still stands 14.9 metres (48.9 feet) high, although it is thought it was once taller perhaps as much as 4.5 metres (15 feet).

The structure lost its roof sometime in the mid to late 19th century. An early 19th sketch shows a stone roof over kirk's nave, chancel and tower.

It is thought that the kirk was built on the spot of an earlier church the one mentioned in the sagas as the site of Earl Magnus' murder in 1115, 1116, 1117 or 1118.

St Olaf's Kirk, Kirkwall

Perhaps one of the most significant historical sites in the town of Kirkwall is also the least known.

Hundreds of people walk past the remains of the St Olaf Kirk daily, the majority of them entirely unaware of its existence and place in the development of the town.

Little remains of the kirk these days, merely a stone archway of cut sandstone found up a lane in the heart of old Kirkwall, a short distance from the harbour.

Founded sometime after 1035, the little church of St Olaf is possibly the original kirk from which Kirkwall took its name *Kirkjuvagr* being the Old Norse name meaning "church bay".

The church was built by Earl Rognvald Brusison who dedicated it to his foster-father, King Olaf Haraldson of Norway. King Olaf was a converted Christian who had died in 1030, at the battle of Sticklastadt.

At this time, Kirkwall was nothing more than two irregular rows of houses. One row spreading from east to west along the shore, the other running southwards at right angles to the sea front and facing the Oyce the area of water now known as the Peedie Sea.

St Olaf's Kirk was then the southernmost building in Kirkwall and attached to an area of consecrated ground that extended to the Papdale burn.

When the remains of St Magnus were moved from Christchurch in Birsay and brought to Kirkwall, it is likely that upon their arrival they were housed within St Olaf's Kirk until the Cathedral, which was under construction, was ready to take them.

The Orphir Round Kirk

During the early period of Norse rule, the Mainland parish of Orphir was a centre of power.

Today, the parish contains the remains of Scotland's only surviving circular medieval church.

Built in the late 11th, or early 12th century, the Orphir Round Kirk is thought to have been built by Earl Hakon. Dedicated to Saint Nicholas, its design was inspired by the Church of the Holy Sepulcher in Jerusalem.

At the time of the kirk's construction, the Great Crusades were in full swing and the circular church had become a popular design with returning crusaders attempting to copy the famous structure in the Holy Land.

Originally, the Round Kirk consisted of a circular nave just over six metres in diameter and an apse. The apse remains today, along with a small section of the nave's eastern section.

It is sad to note that the church survived, almost complete, until the middle of the 18th century when sections were pulled down and the stone used to construct the new parish church. The replacement parish kirk did not last and no trace survives today. The only evidence of its construction is the kirkyard that still surrounds its ancient predecessor.

According to the *Orkneyinga saga*, after the slaying of Saint Magnus in Egilsay, Earl Hakon assumed complete power seizing control of all Orkney.

It is perhaps not surprising that the man responsible for the murder of the beloved Magnus around whose remains strange tales of miraculous happenings were already beginning to circulate was having trouble with his conscience.

The saga explains that as a penance for his terrible crime, Hakon decided to undertake a pilgrimage to the Holy Land. On his return to Orkney, he is said to have instigated the construction of the little church on his estate.

The church is mentioned in the *Orkneyinga saga*, which also tells us that the Earl's drinking hall (or "Bu") stood nearby:

"There was a great drinking-hall at Orphir, with a door in the south wall near the eastern gable, and in front of the hall, just a few paces down from it, stood a fine church. On the left as you came into the hall was a large stone slab, with a lot of big ale vats behind it, and opposite the door was the living room."

The foundations of the Bu were discovered in 1859 (see picture right), although there is some doubt as to whether the kirk and the Bu were in use in the same period.

The saga goes on to recount a number of violent incidents and deaths that took place within this drinking hall. It would appear that these savage bouts of drinking were often interrupted for brief visits to the church.

The Brough of Birsay

Ancient Orcadian seat of Power

For centuries, political and religious power in Orkney centred around a small tidal island off the north-western corner of the Mainland. This island goes by the name of the Brough o' Birsay.

With an area of 21 hectares, the Brough is separated from the Point o' Buckquoy on the Mainland, by the waters of Brough Sound a distance of approximately 240 metres (262 yards).

Access to the Brough is, therefore, restricted to a few hours each day, at either side of low tide, when a causeway across is clear. This not only meant the island had a prime defensive position, but was also an ideal base for sea travel south, north and east.

Originally connected to the Orkney Mainland, the fierce sea erosion, that continues to affect the area, gradually ate away at the land between the Point o' Buckquoy and the island itself. However, although experts are unclear as to when this neck of land was finally severed, it is likely to have been long before the Picts took to the island in the seventh century AD.

The earliest settlement on the Brough is thought to date from the fifth century AD, perhaps Christian missionaries. By the seventh century it was a Pictish stronghold, and by the ninth century had been taken over, and built over, by the Norse.

Most of the remains seen on the Brough today date from its final, Norse, period of use giving buildings ranging from 800-1200AD. This means that, in some cases, different aged remains lie side-by-side, making interpretation of the site by the visitor rather difficult.

The Pictish period

Little remains of the early Pictish settlement on the Brough. When the Norse took over the island, they built their own distinct buildings over the remains of the earlier structures.

Although all that is visible to the modern visitor is a small well and a section of wall, archaeological excavations on the site have revealed the remains of oval shaped Pictish houses thought to date from around 600-700AD.

But despite the lack of Pictish structural remains on the Brough, the wealth of artefacts found indicate the site was once fairly prosperous, perhaps home to an individual or family of considerable status.

Hundreds of fragments of broken moulds, as well as a number of complete moulds, were found on the site. These, together with the crucibles and pieces of worked bronze, confirmed the presence of a metalworker. From the patterns on the recovered moulds it is clear that jewellery typical of the Pictish period was created there.

But of all the Pictish artefacts, undoubtedly one of the most Orkney's most recognisable was uncovered during excavations on the Brough in 1935.

Back then the fragments of a mysterious Pictish symbol stone were unearthed within the area that formed a later Christian kirkyard.

The Pictish Symbol Stone

The solitary symbol stone found on the Brough o' Birsay, is probably the best-known piece of Pictish art found in Orkney.

Thought to date from the eighth century AD, the Birsay stone paints a vivid and intriguing picture of the Pictish nobility who lived in the area.

Originally over six feet tall, the Birsay stone was found in fragments during the 1935 excavation of a later Christian cemetery on the Brough.

How it met its demise is unclear, but it has been suggested that marks on the rear of the stone could indicate that it was deliberately smashed.

Triple grave?

The original stone was removed to a museum in Edinburgh, but a smaller replica stands on the Brough today.

Although the replica is now found within the graveyard, at the head of a triple grave, this is nothing more than "artistic licence" the original stone was found in an area outside the kirkyard wall and is unlikely to have had anything to do with the graveyard.

Pictish symbols

Carved into the stone's face are the fairly common Pictish symbols of a mirror and a crescent and V-rod.

Beneath these is the intriguing creature referred to as the "Pictish Beast" as well as another fine example of the eagle symbol.

Then, at the base of the stone, is a relief depiction of three fully armed Pictish warriors.

Clad in ankle length robes, the three men in the procession carry decorated square shields and massive war spears. Scabbarded around their waists are their swords.

The three men seem to be lined up in order of rank or status the bearded figure at the front is distinctly more ornate and "regal" than his companions.

His cloak is grander, decorated with what appears to be a fringed hem, and his shield is larger and highly embellished. His long, shoulder-length hair is elaborately curled and he may be wearing a head-dress or "crown".

The second man in the line is also bearded but his possessions are nowhere near as grand as his leader. The final warrior is a beardless youth. The impression from the carving is that these two men are definitely subordinate to the lead figure.

What does the stone depict? In truth we will never really know, although we can make suggestions.

It may be that the stone acts as a memorial, perhaps to the warrior "king" shown at the head of the procession.

Or does it commemorate some ancient and now forgotten historical event. Is it a marker stone, designating territory, or simply a piece of decorative art portraying a once common but now lost element of Pictish mythology or folklore.

The Pictish well

Lying to the east of the present day remains of the Norse church is a small, shallow well dating from the Pictish period of the island.

This little well is virtually the only remaining visible evidence that the island once housed a Pictish settlement.

Covered by a slab of stone, the well lies to the east of the main entrance, in an area that later became part of a Norse kirkyard.

A mere 75 centimetres deep, the little well seems to have been closely related to the metalworking that once took place on the Brough.

Constructed from smooth stones from the nearby beach, when excavated it was found to be surrounded by artefacts that linked it to the manufacture of fine metal goods.

These included bronze, glass and crucibles, as well as moulds which confirm that a specifically Pictish style of brooch was once created on the Brough.

These were high-status items and presumaby being made in what was once a high-status settlement.

Although the well may have had a purely practical role in the metalworking process, bearing in mind the suspected Pictish veneration of water and wellsl, it may also have had a more ritual or magical significance.

The Norse Period

Despite the significance the island had to the pre-Norse Orcadians, to the modern visitor it is the later Viking remains that are by far the most prominent.

From the ninth century AD until the twelfth century, the Brough was a Norse settlement and from the gently sloping hillside leading up from the Brough's south-eastern shore are the lower courses of an extensive settlement that includes some of the finest examples of Norse hall-houses so far found in Scotland.

The Brough was perhaps most prominent during the reign of the Norse earl Thorfinn the Mighty (1014-1065) who controlled a vast area extending from Shetland down through the west coast of Scotland and into Ireland.

According to the *Orkneyinga Saga*, Birsay was Thorfinn's seat of power, and tradition has it that the remains of the more elaborate structures on the Brough were once his headquarters.

Between the cliffs and the kirkyard are a series of stone walls that represent different stages of construction at the site, ranging from the 800AD to 1200AD.

The church on the Brough was one of the later additions to the settlement. Built in the twelfth century it was served by a clergy who were housed in purpose-built dwellings to the north of the kirk.

The Norse settlement

The structural remains on The Brough of Birsay show how the site developed throughout the period it was occupied by the Norse from the earliest houses up on the western slope overlooking the settlement to the later, tenth century, structures down by the eastern cliff edges.

The lower courses of the early "hall-houses" are the most numerous their number is slightly misleading to the visitor as they would not all have been in use at the same time.

Built high on sloping ground to the west of the site, the long halls are typical of the period between 800-1000AD.

Built from stone with a turf roof, they were essentially long, rectangular, window-less buildings with central hearths flanked by benches.

These hall-houses were built directly on top of the earlier Pictish buildings, which meant a continuity of settlement stretching over hundreds of years.

By one of these halls are the remains of a byre which would indicate that the early Norse kept at least some of their animals probably sheep on the island itself, rather than on the Mainland.

This may have been the exception to the norm, however, as the animal remains found on the site seems to indicate that livestock was slaughtered off the island with the meat brought in.

Down by the cliffs to the east of the site are the remains of the later Norse houses.

These overlay years of earlier Norse structures dating from the ninth through to the twelfth century AD. The houses visible today date from the tenth century.

The Kirk

The Romanesque church on the Brough of Birsay is by far the best-preserved building on the island.

Its walls survive high enough to allow the visitor to get a good impression of how the building looked when it was in use on the Brough. Dating from around 1100AD, the nave, chancel and apse are still clearly recognisable.

The rectangular nave, the main body of the church, still incorporates a stone bench running around the walls a bench that would have seated those attending the services.

From the nave, a stone step leads through a doorway to the chancel in the eastern end of the building. This small, square room contains the church's altar, although this was reconstructed in the 1930s and may originally have stood in the adjacent apse.

The apse is a semicircular structure attached to the chancel, very similar in design and construction to the Orphir Round Kirk.

The kirkyard

Surrounding the entire church is a stone wall that demarcates the area of the churchyard. This area was used for burials, with a number of stone covered graves still clearly visible to the south of the building.

The Pictish symbol stone was found in this churchyard, directly to the west of the church building.

Foundation remains to the south of the church nave have been interpreted as an earlier church, but there is no evidence to confirm this.

An incompleted tower?

Although nothing survives today, stones jutting from the west wall of the kirk seem to indicate that another structure once stood there, bonded into the fabric of the church.

This structure may have been a square tower, but evidence of this in inconclusive. It may be that the tower was started but never completed.

The lack of medieval finds on the site has led to the conclusion that the church, and adjacent monastery, only remained in use for a short time.

The construction of St Magnus Cathedral in Kirkwall, and the resultant shift of ecclesiastic power away from Birsay could be the reason the site's importance waned.

Was Christ's Kirk on the Brough?

There has been much speculation over the years as to whether the church on The Brough of Birsay was the Christ's Kirk (or Christchurch) of the sagas the burial place of Earl Magnus after his murder on Egilsay.

This seems unlikely, however, as the Place the current Birsay village once contained a considerable medieval church "grander than any other church in Orkney with the exception of only St Magnus Cathedral"

The Monastery

Directly to the north of the church is a range of buildings surrounding a central courtyard. A separate doorway from this courtyard led into the kirk's nave. These buildings were most likely a monastic cloister, housing an order of monks, probably Benedictine or Augustine.

St Magnus Cathedral, Kirkwall

In 1135, Earl Magnus Erlendsson of Orkneywas canonised. About this time, the revered remains of Magnus were taken from Christchurch, in Birsay, where they had lain for 20 years, and moved east.

Their destination was the unassuming little Church of St Olaf, in a small seaside settlement Kirkjuvagr or Kirkwall as it is known now.

Some years later, the saint's relics were moved again this time transferred into the massive, sandstone cathedral that had been raised in Magnus's honour.

The cathedral's founding

The story of the founding of St Magnus Cathedral is well documented within the pages of the *Orkneyinga saga*.

In a tale of political intrigue and dirty deeds, the saga tells us that the cathedral was built on the instructions of Earl Rognvald Kolsson, who had been advised, by his father Kol, to:

"build a stone minster at Kirkwall more magnificent than any in Orkney, that you'll have (it) dedicated to your uncle the holy Earl Magnus and provide it with all the funds it will need to flourish. In addition, his holy relics and the episcopal seat must be moved there."

However, Rognvald's intentions in building the cathedral were not entirely honourable.

Born in Agder, Norway, around 1100AD, Rognvald was the son of Kol and Gunhild, the sister of Saint Magnus. He changed his name from Kali Kolsson in honour of Earl Rognvald Brusison the earl of Orkney from around 1037 until his murder in 1045.

Before long, Rognvald turned his attention to his uncle Magnus's half-share of the Orkney earldom. In 1129, his chance came when he was handed the earldom by the Norwegian king, Sigurd the Crusader.

At the time, Rognvald did nothing about claiming his share. In fact, he did nothing for some time, until King Harald, Sigurd's successor, ratified the claim.

Then, Rognvald assembled a fleet and set sail for Orkney, with the intention of overthrowing Paul Hakonsson, the existing earl of Orkney. After battling severe weather, Rognvald and his men finally landed in the islands, but were met with fierce resistance.

Not surprisingly, Paul had no intention of giving up his earldom without a fight.

It was then that Rognvald's father, Kol, had an idea.

Rather than wage all-out war, he suggested that Rognvald should try and secure the earldom by other, less direct, means. Kol instructed Rognvald to tell the people of Orkney that once he became earl, he would raise the finest church the north had ever seen. This church was to be in memory of his saintly uncle, Magnus, a man whom the islanders venerated above all.

While Rognvald was capturing the hearts of the Orcadian people, behind the scenes he had Earl Paul kidnapped in Rousay and spirited from the islands.

The *Orkneyinga saga* is unclear as to the fate of the dispossessed Paul.

Sweyn Asleifsson is said to have reported back to Rognvald that Paul had been blinded and incarcerated upon the instruction of Paul who had decided to remain in Scotland.

However, it adds:

"But some men tell a story which is less seemly, that Margaret had led Sweyn Asleifsson, by her counsel, to blind earl Paul her brother, and

put him into a dark dungeon; but after that she got another man to take his life there."

The saga concluded:

"...we do not know which of the two stories is more true; but all men know that he never afterwards came back to the Orkneys, nor held he any rule in Scotland."

Paul's murder, or abdication, saw his three-year-old nephew Harald Maddadsson made joint-earl. And back in Orkney, despite the underhand tactics surrounding the fate of Earl Paul, Rognvald was good to his word.

Construction begins

With the earldom in Rognvald's hands, work on the cathedral started. Under the direction of the wily Kol, construction work began in 1137.

The ambitious project was to be built on a prime site by the shore which at that time came up as far as the current Kirk Green.

However, a project on this scale was not cheap and Rognvald's grandiose construction scheme soon ran short of money.

Kol stepped in again, this time advising his son to restore the rights of tenure to Orkney's "ødallers" in return for a cash payment. Rognvald agreed, the scheme was a success and construction continued.

Unfortunately, Earl Rognvald never saw his cathedral reach a state anywhere near completion. In 1158, he was murdered by a rebellious Scottish chieftain.

Holy relics

Rognvald's bones were returned to Kirkwall, where they were eventually placed within the cathedral he had founded.

He was canonised in 1192, but some doubts exist as to the validity of his sainthood, because no existing records seem to confirm it.

However, Saint Rognvald's relics were discovered in the 18th century, set into a stone pillar opposite the one that would, in 1919, be found to contain Saint Magnus' holy remains.

Built from alternating bands of local red and yellow sandstone, the cathedral of Saint Magnus gradually grew, and with it the village at its feet. Upon its completion, three centuries or so after the first foundation stone was laid, it towered over Kirkwall by now a thriving town.

The cathedral has been justifiably described as "one of the finest and best preserved medieval cathedrals in Scotland" and it is not difficult to see why.

Even now, over 860 years after the initial building work began, St Magnus Cathedral still dominates the Kirkwall skyline a familiar, and comforting sight, to Kirkwallians around the world.

Ancient Towns

Stromness The Haven Bay

Around sixteen miles to the west of Kirkwall is Stromness.
Orkney's second main town, Stromness lies on the south western tip of the Mainland, clustered tightly on the shores of Hamnavoe beneath the rocky ridge known as Brinkie's Brae.

Arriving in Orkney from Scrabster, on the Scottish mainland, Stromness is the first port of call. Gliding into the sheltered harbour, the visitor is greeted by a view that has met seafarers for centuries.

The first impression of Stromness is that of an old traditional stone built port, nestling comfortably against the hillside of Brinkie's Brae. Not as old as Kirkwall, Stromness flourished in the 17th and 18th centuries as a result of increased trade with the New World.

The wars between England and France also meant that shipping in the English Channel was dangerous, so the vessels made their way across the north of Scotland and used Stromness as a stop-off point. The ships of the Hudson's Bay Company and the whaling fleets became regular visitors with the town an important recruiting centre for crewmen.

Stromness is similar to Kirkwall in that it follows one long winding road simply known as "the street" also flagstoned, and also shared by pedestrian and motorist.

From this street a great number of narrow lanes and closes branch off. This gives the town a labyrinthine quality with steep narrow paths climbing the hillside on the north side of the street, while on the south, the houses and shops back onto the shore.

However, not all visitors to Stromness we captivated by its charms. When Sir Walter Scott visited Orkney in 1814, he complained that Stromness:

"cannot be traversed by a cart or even by a horse, for there are stairs up and down even in the principal street... whose twistings are often caused by a little enclosure before the house, a sort of yard, about twenty feet square called a park."

Little has changed in central Stromness since Scott's visit. Where once the narrow streets and closes thronged with seamen, whalers and traders now wander tourists, visitors and sightseers.

Kirkwall Orkney's Capital

The capital of Orkney is the Royal Burgh of Kirkwall, a little town on the northern shore of the Orkney Mainland.

Looking out across Kirkwall Bay towards the island of Shapinsay and the outer North Isles, the town sits almost exactly in the centre of the Mainland, neatly dividing it into the distinct areas known simply as the West and East Mainland.

Kirkwall is a town with two faces.

Firstly, there is the face seen by visitors who have travelled there from some urban metropolis. To them it is a small, leisurely town with squat, grey buildings clustered in the shadow of **St** Magnus Cathedral.

The narrow, flagstoned main streets, that serve pedestrian and motorist alike, seems both quaint and unnerving.

The second face is revealed when returning from the North Isles. Approaching from the sea, Kirkwall seems like a bustling city.

Grand buildings decorate the sea-front and the spires of the town's churches challenge the familiar tower of the Cathedral for a place on the skyline. Twisting like an eel, the main street winds from the north to the south, with numerous snaking lanes and closes branching off from the main thoroughfare.

The outskirts of the town may have altered considerably over recent years but the older segments remain practically untouched.

Clustered around these ancient streets are buildings dating from the seventeenth century onward but the oldest surviving buildings to be found within the town are parts of the Bishop's Palace (twelfth century), Tankerness House (which now houses the Orkney Museum and dates from the early sixteenth century) and the Old Kirkwall Grammar School building on Broad Street (sixteenth century).

Kirkwall has a long and colourful history, sadly a fact that most young Kirkwallians now care little about. Over the years, the town's fortunes fluctuated depending upon the varying powers of the islands' earls and bishops who made it their residence.

Kirkjuvagr

Kirkwall is first recorded in the *Orkneyinga Saga* and the town itself probably dates from at least the eleventh century.

At this time, Kirkwall was referred to by its original name *Kirkjuvagr* from the Old Norse meaning 'Church Inlet'. Back then, Kirkwall was merely a cluster of dwellings around a natural harbour formed by the Peerie Sea and the sand bar known as the Ayre.

But contrary to popular belief, the town does not take its name from St Magnus Cathedral but probably the smaller church of St Olaf, the only remainder of which is an unassuming doorway in St Olaf's Wynd an apparently insignificant little lane branching off one of Kirkwall's old main streets.

The Cathedral and the growth of the town

After 1137, once the construction of St Magnus Cathedral was under way, the settlement began to increase in size as craftsmen and artisans moved into the area to work on the new cathedral.

This influx of people settled to the south of the original dwellings, above the shore of the Peerie, now known as Peedie, Sea. At this time, the shore of the Peerie Sea came up the edge of what is now Broad Street, Albert Street and Victoria Street.

The transfer of St Magnus's relics from their previous resting place, Birsay, to St Magnus Cathedral marked the beginning of a new era for the growing town.

From the thirteenth century onward, the process of land reclamation claimed more and more of the area to the west of the old shore. By the 1930s, the shoreline had reached, more or less, its current position.

Royal Burgh

In 1486, King James III of Scotland decreed that Kirkwall be elevated to the status of Royal Burgh.

In his declaration he referred specifically to the two areas of the town known as the Burgh and the Laverock.

The Burgh was the older, northerly section of Kirkwall, the Laverock being the land surrounding the cathedral and under the control of the

Bishop. It is this traditional split between the north and south of the town that may lie at the origin of Kirkwall's annual Ba' games between the Uppies and the Doonies.

Until the early part of this century, Kirkwall comprised of little more than one main street that stretched from the shore and wound its way south, past the front of the Cathedral, and into what is now Victoria Street. This area is still Kirkwall's main commercial centre and known to locals as "up the street" or "doon the toon" depending on the position of your home. The phrase is yet another reminder of the old town split, acted out annually in the Ba' competition.

The Kirkwall Castle was built by Earl Henry Sinclair in the fourteenth century and stood on the site of the existing junction between Albert Street, Castle Street and Broad Street. The castle was destroyed in 1615 after the Sinclair earl and his son rebelled against King James IV of Scotland.

The castle's ruins were finally demolished in 1865. As such, nothing remains of the Kirkwall Castle, apart from a commemmorative plaque on a building in Castle Street

Castles and Strongholds

The Brough of Birsay

Ancient Orcadian seat of Power
For centuries, political and religious power in Orkney centred around a small tidal island off the north-western corner of the Mainland. This island goes by the name of the Brough o' Birsay.

With an area of 21 hectares, the Brough is separated from the Point o' Buckquoy on the Mainland, by the waters of Brough Sound a distance of approximately 240 metres (262 yards).

Access to the Brough is, therefore, restricted to a few hours each day, at either side of low tide, when a causeway across is clear. This not only meant the island had a prime defensive position, but was also an ideal base for sea travel south, north and east.

Originally connected to the Orkney Mainland, the fierce sea erosion, that continues to affect the area, gradually ate away at the land between the Point o' Buckquoy and the island itself. However, although experts are unclear as to when this neck of land was finally severed, it is likely to have been long before the Picts took to the island in the seventh century AD.

The earliest settlement on the Brough is thought to date from the fifth century AD, perhaps Christian missionaries. By the seventh century it was a Pictish stronghold, and by the ninth century had been taken over, and built over, by the Norse.

The remains of the settlement on the Brough of Birsay.

Most of the remains seen on the Brough today date from its final, Norse, period of use giving buildings ranging from 800-1200AD. This means that, in some cases, different aged remains lie side-by-side, making interpretation of the site by the visitor rather difficult.

Cubbie Roo's Castle, Wyre

On the western side of Wyre are the ruins of one Scotland's oldest stone castles.

Known as Cubbie Roo's Castle, the site takes its name from the best-known giant of Orkney folklore. This has led to the widespread connection between the mythical Cubbie Roo and the castle's actual builder, the Norse chieftain, Kolbein Hrúga.

Although there are no distinctive features to allow the experts to conclusively date the structure, it is generally agreed to be have been built around 1145 AD.

This date is corroborated by the *Orkneyinga Saga*, which relates that:

"[Kolbein Hrúga] had a fine stone fort built there, a really solid stronghold"

The island, and its famous castle, is mentioned in other Icelandic sagas, with Kolbein referred to as

"the most haughty of men ...who had a good stone castle built there that was a safe stronghold."

The original structure was a simple stone tower, roughly eight metres square, with walls 1.7 metres thick. A series of ramparts, consisting of a ditch, earthworks and a stone wall, provided the stronghold's outer defences.

Defences

The castle's first line of defence was an earthen rampart encircling a two-metre deep ditch. Those who made it past the ditch would then have been confronted by a towering stone wall.

Today, the wall survives to a height of 1.2 metres but the sheer thickness of its base (2.2 metres) implies that it once rose to a considerable height.

Access to the security of the castle's courtyard was via a "bridge" spanning the outer ditch. This was made up of flat stone slabs laid over two drystane supports.

A second set of supports lie immediately to the north but their function remains unclear.

The castle walls survive to a height of around two metres, with only the ground floor remaining. Given the lack of an entrance in the surviving walls, it seems likely that the entrance to the keep was on a higher level probably the first floor.

Although there is no evidence of an entrance surviving today, an account written in 1688 does make mention of a door high in the walls.

"An unhandy place to attack"

The castle's defences appear to have done their job well.

In *Haakon's Saga*, for example, we learn that it was under siege in 1231 after the murderers of Earl John took refuge there.

Archaeological excavations, in the 1930s, revealed that the stronghold was in use, and maintained, for some time, with at least five external building phases identified. Over time, extensions were added to the main tower and a series of buildings constructed around it.

These external buildings eventually spilled out over the site's defences, which were levelled to make room. This shows that, by this stage of the its development, defence was clearly not as important as it was when the castle was first built.

The Bishop's Palace, Kirkwall

The Bishop's Palace is the older of the two ruined palaces found in the centre of Kirkwall.

Situated a short distance to the south of St Magnus Cathedral, the palace was built in the mid-12th century for Bishop William the Old a friend and crusading companion of Earl Rognvald Kolsson, the cathedral's founder.

The palace was originally intended to provide accommodation for Bishop William and his entourage. So, shortly after the construction work on the cathedral began, the Bishop and his staff moved from their old seat of power in Birsay to their new home in Kirkwall.

At this time, it is likely that the palace conformed to the plan of a Royal Norwegian Palace consisting of a hall, used for entertaining, and a tower house that formed the Bishop's private residence.

King Haakon's base

The first of the "notable" events in the palace's history took place in 1263, over a century after it was first constructed.

Then, the Norwegian king, Haakon the Old, used Kirkwall as a base for his fruitless attempt to maintain Norse rule over the Western Isles.

After a crushing defeat at the Battle of Largs, Haakon's fleet returned to Kirkwall, where the king fell ill.

He died in the Bishop's Palace on December 15, 1263.

By 1320, the palace had been reduced to ruins through neglect. Thereafter, it disappears from the history books, apparently forgotten.

Then, in 1526, the palace came into the possession of William, Lord Sinclair.

His ownership, however, was short lived before he was ordered to return the property to the Bishop of Orkney.

The building returned to prominence in 1540, when King James V of Scotland arrived in Kirkwall and garrisoned his troops in the Kirkwall Castle and the Bishop's Palace.

Soon after, Bishop Robert Reid, the founder of Edinburgh University and the last and greatest of Orkney's medieval Bishops, began an extensive programme of restoration and reconstruction.

Bishop William's restoration

As well as buttressing the palace's badly sagging west wall, Bishop Reid was responsible for the addition of the "Moosie Toor" the strong, round tower at the north-western corner of the palace.

The Moosie Toor, pictured above, still stands today.

In 1568, the ownership of the palace passed to Earl Robert Stewart.

Robert's son, Patrick Stewart, later planned to include the structure in his scheme to build the Earl's Palace, a massive residence in Kirkwall.

But Patrick's plans never came to fruition and, in 1607, "drowned in debt", he was forced to return the complex to Bishop James Law.

In 1614, both palaces were seized by Robert Stewart Earl Patrick's son who staged a rebellion following the incarceration of his father for treason.

This act resulted in a military siege, but whether the action taken against the Stewarts actually damaged the Bishop's Palace is unknown. For more information relating to the events surrounding this siege, see the page dealing with Earl Patrick Stewart.

These days, all that remains of the Bishop's Palace is the shell of one main building and the Moosie Toor. The ruins we see today in no way show the full extent of the building in its heyday.

The Earl's Palace, Birsay

Earl Robert Stewartbuilt the Earl's Palace, in Birsay, between 1569 and 1579.

An illegitimate son of King James V of Scotland, the palace stands monument to Robert's royal pretensions and his oppression of the people of Orkney.

Standing by the shore of Birsay Bay, and dominating the village, the two-storey palace was constructed around a central courtyard and well, with large stone towers at three of the four corners.

These days, the condition of the ruins makes it difficult to imagine how the palace would have appeared in its heyday, but it was an exceptionally fine residence.

But it was as much a fortress as a residence. Only the palace's upper floors had large windows; the accessible ground floors equipped with small openings and an array of gun-holes, from which musketeers could cover every side of the building.

The palace was built in two distinct phases, the first in the 1570s and the second in the 1580s.

The first phase of work saw the construction of the great hall, the principal room of the palace, located initially in the south range and above the main door.

Beside this was Lord Robert's private chamber, in the south-eastern corner tower. An inscription above the entrance, dated 1574, marked this phase.

The second phase probably followed Robert's acquisition of the Orkney Earldom in 1581. This saw the addition of a new range, containing a great hall and chamber, built on the north side of the courtyard.

Few records of the palace remain to give a clear impression of its contents and layout. However, a 1633 account described it as a "sumptuous and stately building", thus confirming it was a luxurious abode.

The Reverend John Brand, who published a description of Orkney in 1701, highlighted the palace's décor, in particular the ceilings, which were elaborated decorated with painting of biblical scenes.

He wrote:

"[The upper floor] hath been prettily decorated, the ceiling being all painted, and that for the most part with schems holding forth scripture histories of Noah's flood, Christ's riding to Jerusalem etc."

After the death of Robert Stewart, the palace was used only occasionally by later earls of Orkney. John Brand's account confirms that by 1701 the palace had begun to deteriorate badly.

The Earl's Palace, Kirkwall

Directly opposite the Bishop's Palace in Kirkwall, and a short distance to the south of St Magnus Cathedral, are the remains of the Earl's Palace.

Hailed as "the finest example of French Renaissance architecture in Scotland", the Earl's Palace is undoubtedly a piece of splendid architectural brilliance.

However, to the people of Orkney, the palace is regarded as a memorial to what has been described as one of the darkest and bleakest episodes of Orkney history the rule of the Stewart Earls.

Patrick Stewart's grand scheme

In the late 16th and early 17th centuries, Orkney was under the rule of the Stewart family, first Earl Robert an illegitimate son of King James V of Scotland and then his son, Patrick. History treats both men as despots and extraordinarily vicious extortioners.

They are alleged to have forced the Orcadians under their rule to work without pay and jailing, or torturing, those who would not comply with their wishes. The Stewarts' men controlled Orkney's council and courts and were therefore held to be above the law.

Then known as the "Newark in the Yards", the construction of the Earl's Palace began in 1600, instigated by Patrick Stewart, a few years after his accession to the earldom. Using forced labour to quarry and ship in the stone for the grandiose scheme, Patrick Stewart planned to build a dwelling unrivalled in design, comfort and beauty.

His plan was to incorporate the remains of the Bishop's Palace into a massive palatial complex. But his dreams were not to be and by 1606, Earl Patrick Stewart was heavily in debt.

The Earl's Palace was completed in 1607 but, shortly afterwards, Patrick Stewart was arrested and work completing the final complex had to be abandoned. After Patrick's execution in 1615, the portion of the Earl's Palace already built became the residence of Orkney's bishops.

Ruination

By 1705, the palace had fallen into disrepair and was no longer fit for habitation. By 1745, the roof had been stripped and the slates sold. The structure has remained roofless ever since.

The Earl's Palace remains a two-storey building today. Consisting of two rectangular sections placed at right-angles to each other, forming an "L" shape, the ground floor contains massive cellars, a large kitchen and a well.

A broad stone staircase leads to the first floor and the main apartments and the great hall.

Measuring over 16 metres long, with two large fireplaces, ornate high vaulted windows and, at the time, sumptuous painted decorations, it is clear to see why the Great Hall was once said to have been one of the finest state rooms of any castle in Scotland.

Outside, the palace entrance was also extremely grand, ornately decorated with tiers of heraldic panels and flanked by carved pillars.

Today, however, the effect is not as impressive Orkney's notorious weather has badly eroded the soft stone used to form the entrance's decorations.

Noltland Castle, Westray

Dating from the 16th century, Westray's Noltland Castle stands testament to a troubled period of Scottish history.

The heavily fortified castle lies approximately half a mile from Pierowall Bay and was built by a Scotsman, Gilbert Balfour from Fife.

Balfour was up to his neck in the political intrigues common during the time of his sister-in-law, Mary Queen of Scots, and as a result had made some powerful enemies.

In 1546 Balfour, along with two of his brothers, was implicated in the murder of Cardinal Beaton. Afterwards, they underwent the siege of St. Andrew's Castle and upon its surrender were sentenced to a period at the oar of a French galley. Balfour's chaplain and partner in crime, John Knox, later described the three brothers as "men without God" who had "neither fear of God nor love of virtue further than their present commodity persuaded them".

In June 1560, Balfour received land from his brother-in-law Adam Bothwell, the Bishop of Orkney. It is thought that work on Noltland Castle began soon after this.

Built from local, grey sandstone, the castle follows as a typical "Z" plan layout, with a rectangular central structure with a square tower position at diagonally opposite corners.

With 7 ft thick walls, Balfour's castle was a stronghold in every sense of the word. The lower floors, have no accessible windows that could be exploited in an assault and are peppered with gunloops 71 in total.

The two towers covered the flanks of the central building, which in turn provides ample opportunity to counter-attack anyone assailing the towers. Built on a slope overlooking Pierowall Bay, anyone approaching the castle, from any direction, would be spotted easily, the multitude of gunloops providing the opportunity to shoot at enemies from any angle.

The main block was designed to have three storeys but was never completed. Although the east end of this structure was roofed, with evidence pointing to prolonged use of the kitchen, the west end was only completed to the second storey and the hall left unroofed. In this respect, the hall probably looks much the same today as it did in the castle's heyday.

The vaulted ground floor contained storerooms and a massive kitchen, with a service staircase leading up to the first floor.

But although the castle was obviously built with defence in mind, it was not entirely spartan, with some more comfortable quarters constructed on the upper floors. The four-storey high north-east tower was completed and served as the residence for the owners, but the south-west tower was left at two floors.

But Balfour's involvement in Mary Queen of Scots' cause was to prove his undoing. In 1571, when support for Mary was on the wane, Balfour was found guilty of treason.

Seeing his opportunity, Lord Robert Stewart, who was later to become Earl of Orkney, then seized Noltland Castle. But Stewart did not hold the property long before he was ordered to hand it back.

But Balfour's problems continued and eventually he was forced to flee to Sweden. There, in 1576, he was executed for his part in an attempt on the King of Sweden's life.

Noltland Castle was then passed to Balfour's nephew, Michael.

The Balfours held Noltland Castle until 1592, when Earl Patrick Stewart, Robert Stewart's son, seized the stronghold as payment for an alleged debt.

In 1606 it became the property of Sir John Arnot, who, after the downfall of Earl Patrick Stewart in 1611, became Sheriff of Orkney.

In the 17th century a range of buildings enclosing a courtyard was added on the south side of the castle. These structures at least were still in use in 1761 when Jerome Dennison of Noltland settled them on his wife, Helen Traill, as part of her marriage contract.

Additions and alterations continued throughout the centuries the castle was in use. Among the most spectacular is the grand staircase, built into the south-west tower, that leads up into the Great Hall. This is thought to have been added by Earl Patrick Stewart.

Today, access to the castle is via this courtyard, the arched entrance of which remains today. On the right hand side of the arch, and barely visible, is inscribed the cryptic message: "When I see the blood I will pass over you in the night."

Archaeological Finds

The Skaill Viking Hoard

In March 1858, a boy named David Linklater chased a rabbit into its hole near St Peter's Kirk in Sandwick. Digging at the entrance to the warren, he came across a few pieces of silver in the earth.

Astounded by the find, young Linklater was soon joined by a number of local folk who had been waiting to gather tangles from the shore of the Bay o' Skaill.

Together, they unearthed, and appropriated, over one hundred items the largest Viking treasure trove found in Scotland to date.

The full story appeared in *The Orcadian* newspaper on March 29, 1858:

Discovery of ancient silver relics

About three weeks ago, a young man found some pieces of silver rings lying near a rabbit hole in the vicinity of the parish church of Sandwick, but took no further notice of the matter, except to acquaint some of his neighbours of it.

On Thursday the 11th inst., a number of persons were down near the church, waiting for the landing of some seaweed, and one of them suggested that they should goand examine the spot where the silver had been found the previous week.

On arriving at the place, one of the men thrust a "ware" fork into the rabbit hole, and drew out a whole parcel of silver fibulae, torcs, etc, and then there commenced a regular scramble, each person endeavouring to secure as much as possible.

Intelligence of the discovery having reached Mr Petrie, clerk of supply, on Saturday morning, the 13th inst., he succeeded, during the day, in obtaining full information on the subject, and, having acquainted Sheriff Robertson with the circumstances, made arrangements to go to Sandwick on Monday morning, to endeavour to secure so valuable a treasure.

On Monday the 15th inst., Mr Petrie went to Sandwick, and, by explaining to the finders the claims of the Crown, and advancing to them £7, and assuring them, farther, that every effort would be made to obtain full remuneration to them, he succeeded in inducing three of the finders of the treasure to hand over to him all that they admitted to be in their custody.

The share found by the fourth party had previously been lodged with his landlord, Mr Irvine, of Quoyloo, by whom it has since been handed over to Sheriff Robertson.

The articles recovered consist of large fibulae, torcs or collars of chain of twisted or rope patterns, armlets or bracelets, and a few coins.

The whole are of silver, and two of the coins are very perfect, and belong to the tenth century; one of them being of the reign of the Anglo-Saxon king, Athelstan, or "Edelstan", about the middle of the tenth century.

It is to be hoped that the officers of Exchequer will act liberally towards the finders of this valuable treasure, so that should any similar discovery be hereafter made, every temptation to concealment of relics of national value, in a historical point of view, may be removed."

Treasure trove

The 15lbs of silver that made up the hoard consisted of nine brooches, 14 necklets, 27 armlets and an assortment of ingots and silver fragments.

There were also a number of Anglo-Saxon and Arabic coins. The fact that many of the objects had been "nicked" presumably to test their quality could indicate that they had passed through a number of hands before ending up in Orkney. In fact, the number of nicks on the items shows roughly how many times each piece had changed owner.

But the treasure did not remain with the finders long. Scots Law dictates that any newly found object is crown property. So, after paying out a reward, Orkney's sheriff clerk at the time, George Petrie, took possession of the priceless hoard.

Eventually, the collection was transferred to Edinburgh where, like most of the important archaeological finds from Orkney, it remains to this day

Norse Hogback Tombstones

One of the most perplexing remnants of the Norse occupation of the islands are the Hogback tombstones.

Found mainly in Northern England and Southern Scotland, the hogback is a three-dimensional house-shaped structure that seem to have been a short-lived monument introduced in the tenth-century by Norse-Irish settlers in North Yorkshire.

Most hogbacks have Christian connections but other than that we know little more.

Of the five hogbacks recorded in Orkney, only four remain and these are likely to be of a considerably later date and are more than likely copies of stones that were encountered in the south.

The Scar Viking Boat Burial

The Discovery
One of Orkney's most important archaeological finds of the 20th century came to light on the island of Sanday after a fearsome storm.

In 1985, while walking along the long, sandy shore at Scar, on the north-western coast of Sanday, a local farmer, the late John Dearness, found a number of bones jutting out from an exposed sandbank.

The ferocity of a storm, a few days previously, had stripped away the side of the bank, revealing the bones. Lying nearby was a small round lead object, about a quarter of an inch in diameter.

Thinking he had stumbled across the grave a sailor who had perished at sea, Mr Dearness picked up the lead object and carried it home. After showing it to a friend, they decided it was simply part of a car battery so it was placed in a kitchen drawer, shut away and forgotten about.

This little lead object proved to be the key to an 1,100 year old mystery.

Significant find

In 1991, after lying hidden for six years, the object was shown to visiting archaeologist, Julie Gibson, who recognised it as a significant archaeological find.

The object was taken back to Kirkwall where it was identified as a lead bullion weight once used by Norse traders to weigh gold and silver on a balance scale.

Excited by the find, Julie Gibson returned to Sanday with Dr Raymond Lamb where they uncovered a few rusty pieces of iron rivet at the site. The true significance of Mr Dearness' chance discovery was rapidly becoming clear.

It looked as though they had found a Viking boat burial.

This instigated a frantic race against time.

With Orkney's notorious autumn storms the Gore Vellyeimminent, an urgent rescue mission had to be mounted before the storms that had revealed the site, returned again and destroyed it.

Historic Scotland acted quickly. A team of archaeologists was sent north to investigate and record the discovery before the rest of the archaeological evidence was washed away for ever.

Their efforts were soon rewarded when the excavation uncovered a pagan Norse boat burial.

Boat to the Otherworld?

Although all wood of the boat had rotted away, the marks left in the sand by over 300 rusted iron rivets marked out the shape of the vessel that had carried its occupants to the Viking otherworld.

The 6.5 metre long boat had been a wooden, plank-built, oared rowing boat of a type known as a faering, but, by the time of the excavation, one side had already been washed away by the fierce tides.

The boat had been buried in a stone-lined pit a pit, the excavations revealed, had been dug too big. Because of this, the vessel had been packed securely into position with stones.

A stone wall had been built across the interior of the boat, forming a chamber of sorts and in this were the remains of three people a man, a woman and a child.

Alongside the human remains was a treasure trove of grave goods objects that were included to accompany the deceased into the afterlife. These objects were unparalleled in Britain both in quality and state of preservation.

Among these discoveries was a decorated whalebone plaque now known as the Scar Plaque and a gilded brooch. Beside the man was an iron sword, a quiver containing eight arrows, a bone comb and a set of 22 gaming pieces.

Alongside the woman was a comb, a sickle, a weaving sword, shears and two spindle whorls.

On the basis of these artefacts and later radio-carbon dating, the grave was dated to between 875 AD and 950 AD.

The Groatsetter Bronze Age Sword

Among the many artefacts uncovered in the parish of St Andrews over the years, a Bronze Age wooden sword is unique in Orkney.

The blade was found in June 1957, near the Tankerness farm of Groatsetter also found recorded as Grotsetter, or Grotster, which are simply transcriptions of the Orcadian pronunciation of the name.

Like the Orkney Hood, the Groatsetter sword was uncovered in a heavily peated area of the parish the anaerobic conditions undoubtedly leading to its remarkable state of preservation.

The farmer of Groatsetter, Mr Robert Petrie, was cutting peats close to the Burn o' Blown, when his tusker (peat cutting tool) struck something solid. Checking the face of the bank he saw what appeared to be a wooden sword securely embedded in the peat over seven feet from the top of the bank.

The leaf-shaped blade was a replica of a Ewart Park type sword a style of early British bronze sword found from 980-790 BC. Measuring 70 centimetres long (2ft 4in), it was carved from yew wood.

As this timber has never grown in Orkney, it would appear that the sword, or at least the timber to create it, was imported.

The sword has been carbon-dated by the National Museums of Scotland and dates from between 900BC and 815BC.

The full length of the sword was 31.3 inches (79.5 cm); what remained of the hilt measured 3 inches (7.6cm). The 'blade' at the thickest part measured 6 inches (15.2cm) in circumference and tapered to thin edges, terminating in a sharp point.

According to *The Orcadian* newspaper on June 20, 1957, the sword:

"has been at one time highly polished, and is in excellent preservation. Part of the handle has been broken off. Dividing the handle from the blade there is a sign of decorative carving."

Although the weapon's "blade" was in a remarkable state of repair, the hilt was considerably worn and polished through repeated use. This seems to imply that although the sword was handled regularly, it was not used for anything that would damage the blade. It continued to be used after the pommel broke off.

So what was the sword for?

It has been suggested that the sword was used as a real weapon an imitation bronze sword in a place where bronze, and bronze artefacts, were relatively scarce. Alternatively, it could have been a wooden practice weapon.

But as you will see from above, the wooden blade was undamaged, which seems to discount any active use as a weapon training or otherwise.

Another possibility is that it was a "master" which was used to create clay moulds for the casting of swords. But why have a mould where there appears to have been a scarcity of bronze? And where are any of the blades made from it? These two questions, together with the fact that any sword made from a mould of the Groatsetter Sword would have been large, unwieldy and used a large amount of precious metal, seems to discount this idea.

The final theory is that it had a ritual, or ceremonial, purpose. Although it may well have been created for the simple purpose of training, somehow it found its way to Orkney, where it may well have assumed the role of a status-symbol. An item carried to impress.

The sword's actual purpose remains lost to time, as do a number of other questions. Was it created in Orkney? Was it a gift? Plundered? Traded?

And was its place in the peat-bog actually an offering to the gods, or was it simply dropped and lost?

Its discovery fits with the idea that water was an element considered special to the early inhabitants of the islands. Was the blade deposited ceremonially in the peat-bog, perhaps as an offering to the spirits, gods or the otherworld?

This is highly possible, given other examples of votive deposits we now know about. One thing is for sure, however. The wear and tear evident on the sword shows it was not created simply for use as an offering. It had been in use for some time, and continued to be used after the hilt broke.

The Orkney Hood

It is rare for organic materials, such as leather, wood or cloth, to survive through the ages. In normal circumstances, they decay rapidly, over a relatively short period of time.

But thanks to the preservative qualities of peat, one of Orkney's most unique discoveries looks almost as good today as when it was created, over 1,700 years ago.

This artefact, a fringed, woollen cloak, now known simply as "the Orkney Hood", is unique among Orkney's many archaeological discoveries. Although countless non-organic artefacts have turned up over the years, it is much rarer to find material or clothing especially in such a superb state of preservation.

In the case of the Orkney Hood, the garment was lost, or deliberately deposited, in a peat bog, and into conditions that ensured its survival for almost two millennia. The lack of oxygen in the peaty conditions of the bog served to practically halt decay.

The circumstances surrounding the discovery of the hood are vague, although it is known that it was found in 1867, near the farm of Groatsetter, in Tankerness. The rare find then managed to find its way into the hands of the National Museum of Scotland (NMS) in Edinburgh where it has remained for well over 100 years.

Radiocarbon-dating by the National Museums of Scotland established that the Orkney Hood dated from between AD250 AD615. Contemporary with the Iron Age site of Minehowe, the garment is probably the oldest, best-preserved sample of textiles in Britain.

The hood is thought to have been made for a child, the fringe along the base originally coming from an adult's garment.

Reconstructing the hood

A replica of the Orkney Hood was recreated in 2002, as part of the Minehowe Knowhow event a combined arts and archaeology interpretation project using Minehowe in Tankerness as a focus.

Following her work recreating the Ice Man's cloak and shoes, for the Bolzano museum in Italy, experimental archaeologist Jacqui Wood was commissioned to create the Orkney replica. Having studied past work on the hood and prepared with sample fleeces and weaving, Jacqui Wood researched the hood at the National Museum of Scotland in Edinburgh, and firmly believed that through the process of recreating the garment that new discoveries will be made about the ancient hood.

She was right, and her educated guesswork paid off with new insights as the replica hood began to take shape.

It proved to be a five-and-a-half-month task of discovery as new facts dawned on her about how the original cape was made and who made it.

Step one was the construction of a prehistoric loom before weaving with the 0.5 millimetre single spun thread.

A report written in the 1950s had suggested how the hood had been constructed, but 40 hours into the job, it became clear that this method was not working the chevron bands across the garment would simply not match up with each other.

"Only by going to the incredible lengths, you really discover what it is really like," explained Jacqui Wood.

"I started measuring the bands and they were not fitting into the original measurements I had taken in Edinburgh. Some of the bands are spun ten rows per centimetre, some eight rows per centimetre, some nine rows per centimetre.

"There are four different thicknesses so some of the bands with more rows were narrower than the bands with less rows."

There could only be one conclusion from her work recreating the hood it began to look increasingly likely that four people had woven the original garment.

"The project took five and half months and a total of 230 hours to actually make it. But it is fascinating to do something like that. It is as important to Britain as the Ice Man's cloak is to Italy. We have not got any garments at all like this, only scraps if we are lucky."

The quality of the original thread of the fringe also pointed to its very high status.

Jacqui believes the fringe possibly belonged to a powerful, wealthy person, that was eventually recycled to make the child's hood. Four eighths of a millimetre threads were spun together to make the half a millimetre thread used throughout the fringe.

"From my own impressions, a mother or father found a very nice quality piece of fabric and made the hood for a child," she said.

The "Orkney Venus"

What was hailed as Scotland's earliest representation of a human was unearthed in Westray in the summer of 2009.

When archaeologists, working at the Historic Scotland excavation at the Links of Noltland, brushed away the mud from a small piece of Neolithic carved sandstone, they saw a face staring back at them.

The human figurine dubbed the "Westray Wifie" by the islanders was described as a "find of astonishing rarity".

Measuring just 41mm tall, 31mm wide and 12mm thick, it is, to date, the only known Neolithic carving of a human form to have been discovered in Scotland with only two other examples in the whole of the British mainland. The only other confirmed figures of a similar era are from
Windmill Hill, in Wiltshire(that has no head), and from Maiden Castle, in Dorset

The Orkney carving is flat, with a round head on top of a lozenge-shaped body. The head has a finely incised M-shaped line across the front which appears to be a brow line. Two parallel vertical lines from the brow to the lower edge seem to be a nose. There are two widely-spaced round dots for eyes, and a possible mouth.

The head is sharply divided from the shoulder line of the torso by a deep groove. The torso expands from the shoulders to the base. What appear to be breasts, or some form of dress fastening, are indicated by fine incision. The right breast is squarer and more emphasised than the left, which is diamond-shaped. A fine, apparently interrupted, V-shaped incised line runs from the right edge of the right breast to the mid-torso and up to the top of the left breast.

Other scratches on top of the skull could be hair, while a clear lattice pattern on the back which might represent textile or clothing, such as a cloak, or, less likely, body decoration.

The Westray figure which was dubbed the "Orkney Venus" by the national media bears some resemblance to the prehistoric "Venus" carvings, from elsewhere in Europe, which have rounded heads, large breasts and exaggerated hips.

According to Richard Strachan, project manager and senior archaeologist with the Historic Scotland cultural resources team, the find was "one of those 'eureka' moments."

He added: "None of the archaeology team have seen anything like it before, it's incredibly exciting. The discovery of a Neolithic carving of a human was quite a moment for everyone to share in."

The building being excavated was once a free-standing farmhouse, surrounded by a wall that was carefully built to look impressive, and standing within a network of fields. After the main period of occupation was over, it appears the farmhouse had secondary, less formal uses perhaps as a store or holding pen for animals.

As the building decayed, it began to fill with rubble and midden. The figurine was found among this midden, suggesting it came from a time after the structure's use as a farmhouse had ended.

Mr Strachan added: "With some of the objects found, you might think they had been left behind, perhaps on a shelf, and just fell down and became buried. But with something this fine, and unusual, it begs the question of whether it may have been deposited there intentionally, perhaps as some act of closure after the building's main use was over."

What the carving was for is uncertain, but it may have had a symbolic purpose the lack of wear and tear suggests it was not regularly handled.

Characters in Orcadian History

Earl Sigurd and the Raven Banner

Earl Sigurd Hlodvirsson is one of the best-known characters in the Orkneyinga Saga. Also known as Sigurd the Stout, he was a powerful man, defending his territories in Caithness against the Scots and renowned for his summertime expeditions plundering the Hebrides, western Scotland and Ireland.

Within the lore of Orkney his prowess is no less. The tales surrounding Sigurd abound with sorcery, miracles and omens. In these stories he is a magical, semi-mythical figure who fights with the power of the Old Gods at his side the last great heathen Earl of Orkney.

To best begin the tale of Earl Sigurd and his magical Raven Banner, I'll leave it to the one who recorded it first the author(s) of the *Orkneyinga Saga*:

"One summer it happened that a Scottish earl called Finnleik challenged Sigurd to fight him on a particular day at Skitten. Sigurd's mother was a sorceress so he went to consult her, telling her that the odds against him were heavy, at least seven to one.

"Had I thought you might live for ever," she said, "I'd have reared you in my wool-basket. But lifetimes are shaped by what will be, not by where you are. Now, take this banner. I've made it for you with all the skill I have, and my belief is this: that it will bring victory to the man it's carried before, but death to the one who carries it."

It was a finely made banner, very cleverly embroidered with the figure of a raven, and when the banner fluttered in the breeze, the raven seemed to be flying ahead. Earl Sigurd lost his temper at his mother's words.

He got the support of the Orkney farmers by giving them back their land-rights, then set out for Skitten to confront Earl Finnleik. The two sides formed up, but the moment they clashed Sigurd's standard-bearer was struck dead. The Earl told another man to pick up the banner but before long he'd been killed too. The Earl lost three standard bearers, but he won the battle and the farmers of Orkney got back their land-rights."

According to the Orkneyinga Saga, five years after the Battle of Svoldr in which King Olaf Trygvasson perished Earl Sigurd left Orkney for the last time, sailing for Ireland with the intention of supporting King Sigtrygg Silk-Beard, the King of Dublin..

In Ireland at the time an internal war was being waged between the King of Leinster and King Brian Boru. These opposing sides were seeking allies so King Sigtrygg, and an alliance of Norsemen, fought with the King of Leinster.

The two sides met on Good Friday, 1014, and Sigurd's Raven Banner was unfurled. The ensuing battle was so fierce that it is said that in places the trees wept blood and the nearby River Tolka turned red.

Within Sigurd's ranks standard bearer after standard bearer fell....

"Then Earl Sigurd called on Thorstein the son of Hall of the Side, to bear the banner, and Thorstein was just about to lift the banner, but then Asmund the White said, "Don't bear the banner! For all they who bear it get their death."

"Hrafn the Red!" called out Earl Sigurd, "bear thou the banner."

"Bear thine own devil thyself," answered Hrafn.

Then the earl said, "`Tis fittest that the beggar should bear the bag;'" and with that he took the banner from the staff and put it under his cloak."

From the moment he touched the standard his fate was sealed. As bearer he was sure to die and he did, impaled shortly afterwards on an enemy's spear.

"There was no man who would bear the raven-standard and the earl bore it himself, and fell there."

Orkneyinga Saga

Back in Orkney there was a man called Hareck who had been ordered by the Earl to stay behind. Hareck reluctantly obeyed but only on the condition that he'd be the first to hear Sigurd's news upon his return.

"He would not that Hareck should go, but said he would be sure to be the first to tell him the tidings of his voyage."
The Saga of Burnt Njal, C157

On the evening of the Battle of Clontarf Hareck saw Sigurd riding home at the head of his warriors. Overjoyed at the return of the Earl, Hareck rode out to greet the returning heroes.

They were seen to meet but then the earth opened and the spectral horde rode under the hill. The hillside closed and Hareck was seen no more.

The Conversion of Earl Sigurd

According to the Orkneyinga Saga, Orkney's conversion to Christianity was achieved in a particularly dramatic fashion.

The tale centres around Olaf Trygvesson, a rich, popular and successful Viking leader, who had been campaigning throughout Britain for several years.

In 995, one year after he had been converted to Christianity himself, Olaf was heading back to Norway with the intention of making a bid for the Norwegian throne.

Leaving Ireland, "Olaf sailed east with five ships and didn't break his journey until he reached Orkney"

In Orkney, he came across Earl Sigurd preparing for a raiding expedition at Osmundwall the place now known as Kirk Hope, in Walls.

The saga recounts:

"Olaf sent a messenger to him, asking Sigurd to come over to his ship as he wanted a word with him.

'I want you and all your subjects to be baptised,' he said when they met.

'If you refuse, I'll have you killed on the spot, and I swear that I'll ravage every island with fire and steel.'

The Earl could see what kind of situation he was in and surrendered himself into Olaf's hands. He was baptised and Olaf took his son, called Hvelp or Hundi, as a hostage and had him baptised too under the name of Hlodvir. After that, all Orkney embraced the faith. Olaf sailed east to Norway taking Hlodvir with him, but Hlodvir didn't Live long and after his death Sigurd refused to pay homage to King Olaf."

The saga does not mention whether Sigurd renounced Christianity after the death of his son, but the accounts of his spectacular later exploits, and death, certainly imply that he remained true to his pagan beliefs

Earl Thorfinn the Mighty

Thorfinn Sigurdsson, or Thorfinn the Mighty, was born around 1009, and, at the height of his power, controlled Orkney, Shetland, the Hebrides, Caithness and Sutherland.

Thorfinn was one of the four sons of Earl Sigurd Hlodvirsson (Sigurd the Stout), who fell at the Battle of Clontarf in Ireland in 1014.

Upon Sigurd's death, the Orkney earldom was left to Thorfinn's brothers, Sumarlidi, Einar "Wry Mouth" and Brusi. Around this time, Thorfinn was made Earl of Caithness and Sutherland by his grandfather, King Malcolm II of Scotland.

After Sumarlidi took ill and died in his bed, sometime around 1015, Thorfinn attempted to claim a share of the Orkney earldom. Einar immediately opposed the move, on the grounds that Thorfinn already held Caithness and Sutherland.

But to keep the peace Brusi eventually gave up his share to Thorfinn, while Einar seized Sumarlidi's third of the earldom and set himself up as overall ruler.

But Einar was overbearing and was not a well-liked man. As a result, his time in control was short. In 1020, Thorkel Amundason Thorfinn's foster-father, killed him in Deerness.

It was Einar's insistence that the Orcadian landowners support his summer raiding campaigns that led to Thorkel first coming up against the Earl. Thorkel, whose father had already refused to speak to the earl, was asked to speak to Einar on behalf of the people of Orkney. So Thorkel approached Einar at a called meeting of landowners, a Thing, and made his plea.

Reluctantly, the earl agreed, but warned Thorkel not to raise the matter again.

The following spring, Einar requested the same level of levy, and again, the Orcadian people asked Thorkel to speak on their behalf. Thorkel agreed, but at the Thing, the earl flew into a rage, forcing Thorkel to flee to Caithness and seek refuge with Thorfinn.

Thorkel remained with the young Thorfinn. He became his foster-father, resulting in him being known thereafter as "Thorkel Fostri" Thorkel the Fosterer.

When Thorfinn came of age, he asked Einar for a share of their father's earldom. Not surprisingly, Einar wasn't keen on the idea. So, Thorfinn massed an army in Caithness ready to take a share by force. In Orkney, Einar was also mobilising troops with the intention of striking Thorfinn first.

But a battle between the siblings was averted.

Brusi, with an army of his own, met Thorfinn and Einar and managed to arrange a bloodless settlement. Thorfinn was granted Brusi's portion of the earldom, while Brusi agreed to share the two thirds held by Einar although Einar would retain leadership with responsibility of defending the islands.

Satisfied, Earl Thorfinn placed men in Orkney to watch over his assets but he remained in Caithness.

Thorkel was regularly despatched back to Orkney to gather Thorfinn's taxes something that rankled Einar, who held Thorkel responsible for Thorfinn's uprising and subsequent acquisition of part of the earldom.

On one such tithe-gathering trip, Thorkel became aware of Einar's plan to assassinate him, but escaped back to Caithness. There, Thorfinn convinced him to travel to the court of the Norwegian king Olaf, rather than confront Earl Einar.

Reluctantly, Thorkel agreed.

During his time in the company of the Norwegian king, Thorkel made sure Olaf was aware of the situation across the North Sea. As a result, the following spring, Thorfinn was brought to Norway to meet the king.

After a successful summer in the Norwegian court, King Olaf gave Thorfinn a fine longship to travel home. Accompanied by Thorkel, he set out for Orkney.

But once alerted to Thorfinn's return, Einar prepared an attack.

Earl Brusi foiled his efforts again, however, arranging a peaceful settlement between the brothers. Part of this was that Einar was to forget his enmity towards Thorkel. To seal the agreement, both men were required to throw a feast for the other.

Thorkel's feast was first, taking place at his Deerness hall at Sandwick. Einar attended, grudgingly, but the peace was kept for a while, at least. Then, on the day the Earl was due to leave, with Thorkel in attendance, Thorkel sent men ahead to scout out the road. They returned with the news that three ambushes awaited.

Upon hearing this, Thorkel gathered his men.

Then, when Einar's retinue announced it was time to leave, Thorkel declared that he was not yet ready and made his way to the main hall. Entering, he closed the door and went to where Einar sat by the fire.

"Are you ready?" snapped the Earl.

"I am ready," replied Thorkel, and with a single blow to the head, killed Einar, sending his corpse tumbling forwards into the fire.

After Einar's murder, Brusi took control of his lands, thus assuming control of two thirds of the earldom. Thorfinn questioned this, feeling they should have equal shares.

Brusi knew he could not withstand an assault by his brother' and his allies, so instead sought the assistance of King Olaf of Norway. But Olaf was shrewd, and awarded himself Einar's third, over which he made Brusi steward.

When Thorfinn arrived in Norway, with the intention of petitioning the king for aid, Olaf presented him with the same choice hand over the earldom and declare himself "the King's man".

Diplomatically, Thorfinn refused, stating that he was already bound to owe allegiance to his grandfather, the King of Scotland. However, acting on advice from Thorkel, Thorfinn eventually agreed to King Olaf's terms.

As a result, Brusi and Thorfinn were to hold a third of the earldom each, with Olaf claiming he would maintain a third himself. But the king was obviously wary of Thorfinn's ambitions . After the young earl's departure for Orkney, the King awarded a second third to Brusi, whose son Rognvald remained at the Norwegian court.

After leaving Norway, however, Thorfinn spent little time in Orkney, once again leaving retainers to look after his interests in the earldom.

Because of Thorfinn's absence, the responsibility for defending the territory fell on Brusi's shoulders. And he was struggling under a constant stream of raids. Brusi complained to his brother that he was doing nothing to defend his share, although he was keen enough to gather the taxes due to him.

So Thorfinn made an offer. If Brusi granted him two thirds of the earldom, he would assume sole responsibility for the defence of the islands.

And so the overall power in the earldom of Orkney passed to Earl Thorfinn

Magnus the Martyr of Orkney

The story of Magnus Erlendsson Orkney's Saint Magnus begins in 1098 a time when the Orkney earldom was divided between two brothers, the earls Paul and Erlend.

Magnus was the eldest son of Earl Erlend, while his cousin, Hakon, was the son of Paul.

In 1098, the Norwegian king, Magnus "Barelegs", arrived suddenly in Orkney, where he unseated both earls and made his illegitimate son, Sigurd, overlord of the islands.

Earls Paul and Erlend were instructed to go to Norway, where they both died before winter's end.

With Sigurd in place as "king" of Orkney, King Magnus left Orkney on a raiding expedition, making sure he took Hakon and the 18-year-old Magnus with him.

Heading down the west coast of Scotland, the raiders travelled as far south as Anglesey.

The raid on Anglesey

According to the sagas, on the voyage south young Magnus would not fight during the raids.

When the Vikings attacked the Welsh rulers of Anglesey, for example, Magnus refused to participate. Instead, we are told he chose to remain on the ship singing psalms.

This overtly Christian behaviour did not please the Norwegian King, who already disliked Magnus intensely and regarded him a coward.

This episode, although perfectly setting up the saintly image of Magnus, could have a number of explanations.

Firstly, it is highly possible that the account is a later addition, specifically introduced to emphasise Magnus' piety. The lack of references to Magnus in other historical accounts of the raiding voyage has prompted suggestions that his inclusion in the *Orkneyinga saga* version of events was purely fictional.

However, if we assume that Magnus was part of the raiding party, his refusal to fight could have been for purely political reasons rather than spiritual.

The historian William Thomson points out in his *New History of Orkney*, that Magnus had a "surprisingly frequent involvment in Welsh affairs".

Whatever the truth, the *Orkneyinga saga* goes on to explain that Magnus escaped from the king's ship. Slipping overboard one night, he swam to the shore of Scotland, where he "disappeared" until the death of King Magnus in Ireland in 1102.

We know little about this time in hiding.

Earl Harald and the Poison Shirt

During the reign of the brothers Harald and Paul, a Christmas feast was arranged at Earl Harald's estate in Orphir and, as he was to provide for them both, he was busy with the preparations.

Their mother Helga and her sister Frakokk were staying there at the time and happened to be sitting in a small room getting on with their needlework, when Earl Harald came into the room. The sisters were sitting on the cross-dais and a newly made linen garment, white as snow, was lying between them. The Earl picked it up and saw that in many places it was stitched with gold thread.

"Whose is this treasure?" he asked.

"It's meant for your brother Paul," answered Frakokk.

"Why take such pains making clothes for him?" asked the Earl, "You're no so particular when you make mine!"

The Earl had only just got up and was wearing nothing but a shirt and linen breeches, with a tunic thrown over his shoulders. He cast it off and began unfolding the linen garment, but his mother grabbed hold of it and told him that there was no reason to be envious just because his brother had some fine clothes. The Earl snatched it back and was about to put it on when the sisters pulled off their bonnets, tore their hair and said that if he put on the garment his life would be at risk. Though they were both in tears he didn't let that stop him, but no sooner was the garment upon his back than his flesh started to quiver and he began to suffer terrible agony. He had to go to bed and not long after that he died. His death was deeply mourned by his friends.

Immediately after Harald's death, his brother Paul took over the entire earldom with the approval of every farmer in Orkney Earl Paul realised that the precious robe put on by Earl Harald had been meant for himself and for that reason he would not let the sisters stay on in the islands, so they went off with all heir dependants, first across to Caithness and from there to Frakokk's estates in Sutherland.

It was there that Frakokk reared Erlend, the son of Harald Smooth-Tongue, while he was still a boy. There was another boy there too, Olvir Brawl, the son of Thorljot of Rack Wick and Steinvor Frakokk's-daughter. He grew to be an exceptionally big and powerful man, a great troublemaker and a killer.

Others brought up there were Thorbjorn Clerk, son of Thorstein the Yeoman and Gudrun Frakokk's-Daughter, Margaret the daughter of Earl Hakon and Helga Moddan's-Daughter, and Eirik Stay-Brails. All these people were high-born and thought well of themselves. They all believed that they had a just claim on the earldom of Orkney which had once belonged to their kinsman Earl Harald. Frakokk had two brothers, Angus the Generous and Earl Ottar of Thurso, a man of great character.

Kolbein Hruga The original Cubbie Roo?

"Vigr was the homeland of that famous Orkneyman Kolbein Hrúga. In the traditions of the natives, Kolbein became a fabulous personage, a giant who cast stones at rocks at churches."

Kolbein Hrúga was a Norse chieftain who settled in Orkney some time around 1142. Described by the Orkneyinga Saga as "most outstanding of all men", Kolbein was born in Sunnfjord, Norway.

Around 1145, shortly after arriving in Orkney, Kolbein was responsible for the construction of a stronghold on the island of Wyre.

"At the time there was a very able man called Kolbein Heap farming on Wyre in Orkney. He had a fine stone built fort, a really solid stronghold."

Kolbein's fort, the remains of which are now commonly known as Cubbie Roo's Castle, is one of the earliest stone built castles in Scotland and is certainly regarded as the best preserved. It obviously saw some action in its time as it gets a mention in the pages of *Haakon's Saga*. It recounts that Kolbein's stronghold was a difficult place to attack.

Kolbein was undoubtedly a large, powerful man, attested by the fact that "Hrúga" means "Heap" in Old Norse.

From the few mentions he gets in the *Orkneyinga Saga,* we can see that he was a man of some influence. Indeed, it was with Kolbein's help that King Eystein gained his kingship.

One of Kolbein's sons, Bjarni, became Bishop of Orkney and may have inaugurated the Kirkwall Grammar School.

Bjarni was responsible for the relocation of the remains of the murdered Earl Rognvald from Caithness to their final resting place in the St Magnus Cathedral.

Sweyn Asleifsson 'The Ultimate Viking'

Of all the characters in the Orkneyinga Saga, it is perhaps Sweyn Asleifsson who has come to personify the archetypal Viking.

Christened the "Ultimate Viking" by the Orkney writer Eric Linklater, Sweyn Asleifsson comes across in the saga as a charismatic, but ruthless, character.

He was undoubtedly a fearsome warrior, although it is through cunning and tactics that he often triumphed. He was firmly entangled in the shifting politics of the 12th century Orkney Earldom and although a fierce ally, switched allegiances almost at a whim.

Sweyn used his homeland in Orkney, and properties in the Western Isles of Scotland, as bases to launch raids on the rest of the British Isles.

Concentrating on farming in the summer, Sweyn was like a number of other chieftains who went raiding whenever convenient.

According to the *Orkneyinga saga*:

"This was how Svein used to live. Winter he would spend at home on Gairsay, where he entertained some eighty men at his own expense. His drinking hall was so big, there was nothing in Orkney to compare with it. In the spring he had more than enough to occupy him, with a great deal of seed to sow which he saw to carefully himself. Then when

that job was done, he would go off plundering in the Hebrides and in Ireland on what he called his 'spring-trip', then back home just after mid-summer, where he stayed till the cornfields had been reaped and the grain was safely in. After that he would go off raiding again, and never came back till the first month of winter was ended. This he used to call his 'autumn-trip'."

Sweyn was born sometime before 1135, the son of Olaf Hrolfsson of Gairsay and Asleif.

His father was murdered in 1135, by Olvir Rosta, a chieftain from Sutherland, who was seeking revenge after being soundly defeated by Olaf in a sea battle off the coast of Tankerness. Olvir had launched a surprise raid on Olaf's residence in Caithness, in the north of Scotland, where he burned the house down around the warrior's head.

Later that year, during Earl Paul's Yule feasts at his Bu (hall) in Orphir, an exchange of insults between Sweyn Asleifsson and Sweyn Breastrope, a colleague of Asleifsson's father, the hot-headed young Sweyn killed Breastrope.

Outlawed by Earl Paul, Sweyn fled to the island of Egilsay, where he was despatched to the Scottish island of Tiree, on the west Coast of Scotland, by Bishop William the Old. There, Sweyn was given refuge by a chieftain referred in the saga only as Holbodi.

Back in Orkney, in 1136, Sweyn managed to kidnap Earl Paul on the island of Rousay, spiriting him away and leaving the Earldom open for Rognvald II to step in and assume control. Upon his return to Orkney, Sweyn's forfeited lands were returned by the new Earl.

In 1139, having assisted Rognvald in his efforts to gain the Earldom, Sweyn set about paying off some of his own private scores. Seeking revenge for the death of his father, Sweyn concentrated first on Olvir Rosta. To carry this out, Sweyn asked Earl Rognvald for two fully manned ships, a request the Earl granted.

Sweyn then sailed south and into the Moray Firth, intending to launch a surprise attack on Olvir Rosta's residence at Helmsdale in Northern Scotland. He landed to the south of Helmsdale and, acquiring men and guides from Earl Maddad, headed north to finally avenge his father.

Expecting the assault from the north, Olvir had concentrated his forces to the north of his lands and was therefore caught unawares. A short fight took place and Olvir's forces were routed. Olvir himself fled up the valley and escaped to the Western Isles, leaving Sweyn's men ransack the house before setting it alight and burning all the inhabitants, including Olvir's mother Frakkok.

After plundering the area, Sweyn returned to his ships and sailed back to Orkney where Earl Rognvaid "received them cordially."

In 1140, Sweyn sailing southwards again, this time to go to the aid of his comrade, Holbodi of Tiree.

While wintering at Duncansby in Caithness, a messenger had come from Holbodi asking for help against a group of Welsh marauders who had burned down his house.

Sweyn again approached Earl Rognvald asking for ships and men. His request granted, he sailed west and drove the Welshmen from Tiree, pursuing them as far as the Isle of Man. There the Welsh warriors escaped but not before killing Andres, a local chieftain.

Andres had been a man of some wealth and considerable estates. Following his death, his widow, Ingirid, was now a prize to be sought after. Sweyn asked for Ingirid's hand in marriage, but she would not consent unless he he avenged her former husband's death.

Sweyn agreed and, accompanied by Holdbodi and five ships, spent the summer raiding the coasts of Wales. Failing to capture the warband that had slain Andres, Sweyn returned to the Isle of Man where he married Ingirid and settled down for the winter.

The spring of 1141 saw Sweyn on the move again, but Holbodi, who was now allied to the Welsh, did not join him.

Sweyn made for Ireland, returning home in the autumn, laden with booty. In the winter Holbodi and his men attacked Sweyn's house in Man but were repelled. Now wary of the Hebrideans, Sweyn relocated to Lewis in the Western Isles, where he remained until 1143, when he returned to Orkney, and his family seat in Gairsay.

During Sweyn's time in the Western Isles, the Earl of Orkney, Rognvald, had become friendly with a man called Thorbjorn Klerk. Thorbjorn was one was of the men who had stood with Olvir when Sweyn had attacked his estate some years previously.

Rognvald sailed to Gairsay and succeeded in reconciling Sweyn and Thorbjorn. And for a time all was well between the two men.

But Holbodi's treachery was not forgotten and Sweyn once again approached the Earl looking for men and ships. Rognvald provided five vessels, and with Thorbjorn Klerk at the helm of one of the vessels, Sweyn's fleet set sail for Tiree.

Undoubtedly sensing his doom, Holbodi fled Tiree, leaving Sweyn and his allies free to loot the island. They accrued considerable plunder and agreed that their spoils should be divided equally.

But Sweyn demanded a chief's share.

This caused unease among the other captains, and after Thorbjorn complained to Earl Rognvald, the Earl made up the captains' loss with money from his own treasury. Thorbjorn took the Earl's money but his friendship with Sweyn was ended.

During Sweyn's time in the Western Isles, he had left a man called Margad to manage his estates in Caithness. Margad, however, was somewhat tyrannical and succeeded in stirring up trouble among the people. On Sweyn's return, Margad slew a neighbouring chieftain, Hroald, in Wick, knowing well that this act would cause trouble. Sweyn gathered up sixty men including Margad and retired to the tower of Lambaborg and prepared for a siege.

Earl Rognvald, at the request of Hroald's son, gathered a force and laid siege to Lambaborg, demanding the surrender of Margad. Sweyn refused to give him up, so the siege continued.

As part of a daring escape plan, Sweyn instructed his men to gather all the ropes they could find and knot them together. Then, under cover of the night, Sweyn and Margad were lowered into the sea below the fortress. Swimming to safety, they escaped southwards, eventually ending up at the court of King David of Scotland.

King David managed to reconcile Earl Rognvald and Sweyn and eventually the "Ultimate Viking" returned home to Orkney.

Earl Sigurd the Powerful

The first earl of Orkney

According to the Orkneyinga Saga, Sigurd Eysteinsson or Earl Sigurd the Powerful was the first Earl of Orkney.

But although the saga makes it clear that Earl Sigurd I was one of the three great earls of Orkney, it actually documents very little of his reign.

Sigurd enters the saga as the forecastleman of one of King Harald Fairhair's ships, on the voyage of conquest to Orkney, Shetland and the Western Isles.

According to the saga, the Norwegian king had sailed westwards to deal with Vikings who, after raiding Norway throughout the summer, were making the Northern Isles their base.

Harald's forces conquered Orkney and Shetland before going on to the Hebrides and the Isle of Man.

During this voyage, Sigurd's brother, Earl Rognvald of More, received the Earldom of Orkney from King Harald as compensation for the loss of his son, Ivar.

Sigurd gains the earldom

Rognvald had no intentions of staying in the islands so passed the earldom to Sigurd, who became Earl Sigurd I of Orkney. As earl, Sigurd ruled wisely and became very powerful but unfortunately the saga says little more of his reign.

Instead the reader is hurled into the tale of Earl Sigurd's death a story that remains firmly in the memories of Orcadians today, as a folkloric origin for the Kirkwall Ba' game.

Earl Sigurd had formed an alliance with Thorstein the Red, travelling south into Scotland where they conquered all of Caithness and large parts of Argyll, Moray and Ross.

Glossing over the exact details of the campaign, the saga goes on to tell us that Earl Sigurd constructed a stronghold in Moray before mentioning a feud between Sigurd and a local magnate Maelbrigte.

The reason for the two men's enmity is not given, but it was undoubtedly to do with the Orkney earl's forays into Scottish territory. Whatever the cause, both men agreed they should meet to settle their differences, each taking no more than forty men.

Sigurd, however, decided that the Scots were not to be trusted so turned up to the "meeting" with eighty warriors two warriors mounted on each of his forty horses.

Orcadian treachery

Maelbrigte was aware that treachery was afoot when he noticed that there were two feet on each side of every Orkneyman's horse. Knowing he had been betrayed by the Orkney earl, he instructed his men to fight on and slay two of the enemy each. A battle ensued and, despite their bravery, the outnumbered Scottish side perished and Maelbrigte was slain.

Elated at his victory, Sigurd had the heads of his vanquished enemies severed and, as a show of triumph, strapped to each of his warriors' saddles.

Snatching up his own grizzly trophy, Sigurd fastened Maelbrigte's head to his saddle. The earl's forces then headed back north but Maelbrigte had his revenge. While spurring his horse during the ride home, Earl Sigurd's leg was scratched by Maelbrigte's protruding buck-tooth.

Sigurd's Howe

The scratch became infected and before long Earl Sigurd the Powerful died.

He was buried at "Ekkjalsbakki" the banks of the River Oykell in Scotland. Although the exact location is unknown, the area of Earl Sigurd's burial place is now known as Ciderhall a corruption of the Norse words meaning "Sigurd's Howe".

See side panel for further details.

His son, Guthrom, ruled the earldom for one winter before dying childless. Earl Rognvald of More's son was then sent from Norway to become earl.

Events in Orkney's History

The Viking Days of the Earldom

The Death of King Haakon

In 1263, the Norwegian king Haakon the Old used Kirkwall as a base for his fruitless attempt to maintain Norse rule over the Western Isles.

After his crushing defeat at the Battle of Largs on October 2, 1263, Haakon's battered fleet returned to Kirkwall, where the King fell ill and died in the Bishop's Palace.

The events surrounding King Haakon's death are detailed in full within *Haakon Haakonsson's Saga*:

"King Haakon had spent the summer in much watchfulness and anxiety. Being often called to deliberate with captains, he had enjoyed little rest; and when he arrived at Kirkwall, he was confined to his bed by his disorder. Having lain for some nights, the illness abated, and he was on foot for three days.

On the first day, he walked about in his apartments; on the second, he attended at the Bishop's chapel to hear mass; and on the third he went to Magnus's church, and walked round the shrine of St Magnus, Earl of Orkney.

He then ordered a bath to be prepared, and got himself shaved. Some nights after, he relapsed, and took again to his bed.

During his sickness, he ordered the Bible and Latin authors to be read to him. But finding his spirits were too much fatigued by reflecting on what he had heard, he desired Norwegian books might be read to him night and day: first the lives of saints; and, when they were ended, he made his attendants read the chronicles of our Kings from Halfdan the Black, and so of all the Norwegian monarchs in succession, one after the other.

The King still found his disorder increasing. He therefore took into consideration the pay to be given to his troops, and commanded that a mark of fine silver should be given to each courtier, and half a mark to each of the masters of the lights, chamberlains, and other attendants on his person.

He ordered all the silver plate belonging to his table to be weighed, and to be distributed if his standard silver fell short.

At this time also letters were written to Prince Magnus concerning the government of the nation, and some things which the King wanted to have settled respecting the army.

King Haakon received extreme unction in the night before the festival of St Lucy. Thorgils Bishop of Stavanger, Gilbert Bishop of Hamar, Henry Bishop of Orkney, Abbot Thorleif, and many other learned men were present; and before the unction all present bade the King farewell with a kiss.

He still spoke distinctly; and his particular favourites asked him if he left behind him any other son than Prince Magnus, or any other heirs that should share in the kingdom, but he uniformly persisted that he had no other heirs in the male or female line than were publicly known.

When the history of all the Kings down to Sverrir had been recited, he ordered the life of that Prince to read, and to be continued night and day, whenever he found himself indisposed to sleep.

The festival of the Virgin Lucy happened on a Thursday, and on the Saturday after, the King's disorder increased to such a degree that he lost the use of his speech; and at midnight* Almighty God called King Haakon out of this mortal life. ...Immediately on the decease of the King, Bishops and learned men were sent for to sing mass. Afterwards all the company went out except Bishop Thorgils, Brinjolf Johnsson, and two other persons, who watched by the body, and performed all the services due to so illustrious a lord and prince as King Haakon had been.

On Sunday the royal corpse was carried into the upper hall, and laid on a bier.

The body was clothed in a rich garb, with a garland on the head, and dressed out as became a crowned monarch. The masters of the lights stood with tapers in their hands, and the whole hall was illuminated.

All the people came to see the body, which appeared beautiful and animated, and the King's countenance was fair and ruddy as while he was alive.

It was some alleviation of the deep sorrow of the beholders to see the corpse of their departed sovereign so decorated."

Earl Harald and the Poison Shirt

During the reign of the brothers Harald and Paul, a Christmas feast was arranged at Earl Harald's estate in Orphir and, as he was to provide for them both, he was busy with the preparations.

Their mother Helga and her sister Frakokk were staying there at the time and happened to be sitting in a small room getting on with their needlework, when Earl Harald came into the room. The sisters were sitting on the cross-dais and a newly made linen garment, white as snow, was lying between them. The Earl picked it up and saw that in many places it was stitched with gold thread.

"Whose is this treasure?" he asked.

"It's meant for your brother Paul," answered Frakokk.

"Why take such pains making clothes for him?" asked the Earl, "You're no so particular when you make mine!"

The Earl had only just got up and was wearing nothing but a shirt and linen breeches, with a tunic thrown over his shoulders. He cast it off and began unfolding the linen garment, but his mother grabbed hold of it and told him that there was no reason to be envious just because his brother had some fine clothes. The Earl snatched it back and was about to put it on when the sisters pulled off their bonnets, tore their hair and said that if he put on the garment his life would be at risk. Though they were both in tears he didn't let that stop him, but no sooner was the garment upon his back than his flesh started to quiver and he began to suffer terrible agony. He had to go to bed and not long after that he died. His death was deeply mourned by his friends.

Immediately after Harald's death, his brother Paul took over the entire earldom with the approval of every farmer in Orkney Earl Paul realised that the precious robe put on by Earl Harald had been meant for himself and for that reason he would not let the sisters stay on in the islands, so they went off with all heir dependants, first across to Caithness and from there to Frakokk's estates in Sutherland.

It was there that Frakokk reared Erlend, the son of Harald Smooth-Tongue, while he was still a boy. There was another boy there too, Olvir Brawl, the son of Thorljot of Rack Wick and Steinvor Frakokk's-daughter. He grew to be an exceptionally big and powerful man, a great troublemaker and a killer.

Others brought up there were Thorbjorn Clerk, son of Thorstein the Yeoman and Gudrun Frakokk's-Daughter, Margaret the daughter of Earl Hakon and Helga Moddan's-Daughter, and Eirik Stay-Brails. All these people were high-born and thought well of themselves. They all believed that they had a just claim on the earldom of Orkney which had once belonged to their kinsman Earl Harald. Frakokk had two brothers, Angus the Generous and Earl Ottar of Thurso, a man of great character.

Magnus the Martyr of Orkney

The story of Magnus Erlendsson Orkney's Saint Magnus begins in 1098 a time when the Orkney earldom was divided between two brothers, the earls Paul and Erlend.

Magnus was the eldest son of Earl Erlend, while his cousin, Hakon, was the son of Paul.

In 1098, the Norwegian king, Magnus "Barelegs", arrived suddenly in Orkney, where he unseated both earls and made his illegitimate son, Sigurd, overlord of the islands.

Earls Paul and Erlend were instructed to go to Norway, where they both died before winter's end.

With Sigurd in place as "king" of Orkney, King Magnus left Orkney on a raiding expedition, making sure he took Hakon and the 18-year-old Magnus with him.

Heading down the west coast of Scotland, the raiders travelled as far south as Anglesey.

The raid on Anglesey

According to the sagas, on the voyage south young Magnus would not fight during the raids.

When the Vikings attacked the Welsh rulers of Anglesey, for example, Magnus refused to participate. Instead, we are told he chose to remain on the ship singing psalms.

This overtly Christian behaviour did not please the Norwegian King, who already disliked Magnus intensely and regarded him a coward.

This episode, although perfectly setting up the saintly image of Magnus, could have a number of explanations.

Firstly, it is highly possible that the account is a later addition, specifically introduced to emphasise Magnus' piety. The lack of references to Magnus in other historical accounts of the raiding voyage has prompted suggestions that his inclusion in the *Orkneyinga saga* version of events was purely fictional.

However, if we assume that Magnus was part of the raiding party, his refusal to fight could have been for purely political reasons rather than spiritual.

The historian William Thomson points out in his *New History of Orkney*, that Magnus had a "surprisingly frequent involvment in Welsh affairs".

Whatever the truth, the *Orkneyinga saga* goes on to explain that Magnus escaped from the king's ship. Slipping overboard one night, he swam to the shore of Scotland, where he "disappeared" until the death of King Magnus in Ireland in 1102.

We know little about this time in hiding.

Scottish Rule

The Battle of Summerdale

The Battle of Summerdale, in 1529, as any Orcadian should be able to tell you, was the last pitched "battle" fought on Orkney soil.

Although history, and local tradition, treats the confrontation as a battle, it was more likely to have been a brief, bloody, skirmish on the boundary of the parishes of Orphir and Stenness.

After the transfer of Orkney to the Scottish Crown in 1468, the former Earldom property was rented to tacksmen. These individuals collected the various skats, rents and other dues formerly paid to the Earls. Needless to say, some of the tacksmen were disliked and, in some cases, used their power unscrupulously.

In 1489, Lord Henry Sinclair, was tacksman. After his death at the Battle of Flodden, the tack was allowed to pass to his widow.

Henry's son, William, was a minor at the time of his father's death, so his uncle, Lord William Sinclair of Warsetter, took over Henry's legal duties. On Warsetter's death, young William Sinclair was made Justice Depute of Orkney, but his behaviour soon led to trouble and eventually a revolt.

The Sinclair uprising

A body of udallers, led by James Sinclair of Brecks, refused to pay dues for three years. These men, who feared the encroachment of Scottish feudalism into Orkney, rebelled.

James Sinclair, aided by his brother Edward (both illegitimate sons of Sinclair of Warsetter), led the uprising that led to the seizure of the Kirkwall Castle, the Sinclair stronghold.

A number of people were killed during the incident and William Sinclair fled from Orkney to take up refuge in Caithness.

There, the exiled Sinclair made an appeal to the Crown, asking for assistance to quash the rebellion in Orkney. The following year, a Royal demand was made to the insurgents to hand over the castle.

They refused.

So, acting on Royal authority, William Sinclair, with the help of his kinsman John, Earl of Caithness, raised a force of around 500 men from Caithness and invaded Orkney.

According to Orcadian tradition, the invading force landed in the parish of Orphir, on the north side of Scapa Flow. But Sir James Sinclair, well aware that they were approaching, had gathered a large body of Orcadians to resist the invaders.

Many traditional stories about the battle have been handed down over the ages.

The witch's prophecy

It was said that when the Earl of Caithness and his troops landed in Orphir, a witch walked before them on the march.

The crone unwound two balls of wool one blue, the other red. The red ball was the first to run out and the witch assured the Earl that the side whose blood was spilled first would certainly be defeated.

It would appear that the Earl put great faith in the witch's proclamation. So much so that he was determined to slay the first Orcadian he met man, woman or child to ensure his victory on the day.

The first person he met was a defenceless young herd boy. The Caithness men fell on the hapless youth and murdered him. Only after the lad lay dead at their feet did they learn from the witch that their victim was no Orcadian he was a Caithness boy who had taken refuge in Orkney.

Unnerved by the incident, if tradition is to be believed, the Caithness men's actions had a major effect on their conduct at the battle.

The battle by the loch

The Earl's men marched up the valley on the west side of the Loch o' Kirbister, while James Sinclair's Orkney rebels followed a route to the east side of the loch.

The two forces met at the valley of Summerdale and in the clash that followed, tradition says that the invaders were completely routed. They cast their weapons into the Kirbister Loch and fled the carnage. But the few who survived the battle were pursued as they ran back to their boats and slaughtered.

The Earl himself reached the farm of Oback and dashed in among the farm buildings to seek a hiding place, only to be met by a party of his enemies who slew him on the spot. It was said that the Earl's head was sent back to Caithness in defiance.

Only one Orkneyman is said to have been killed on that day. His death was a tragic one; after the battle he dressed himself in clothes taken from a dead Caithness man and on his return home his mother, thinking he was one of the enemy, struck him on the head with a makeshift weapon a stone in the foot of a stocking.

James Sinclair's pardon

But despite Sir James Sinclair blatant defiance of the Crown, the King of Scotland not only pardoned him but also gifted him a feudal grant of the islands of Sanday and Stronsay.

Some maintain that this act of appeasement was made in order not to drive the islanders into the arms of King John of Norway and Denmark, who had pledged himself to redeem the mortgaged islands.

The Sixteenth Century

The Westray Dons and the Spanish Armada

There can be few people who don't know the story of the English nobleman, Sir Francis Drake, and the Spanish Armada.

When the Armada was sighted on July 19, 1588, Drake was playing a game of bowls on Plymouth Hoe in England. Legend has it that he finished his game boarding his vessel, the *Revenge*.

But although this historical tale of the Spanish Armada is well-known, few outside Orkney know the historical impact the Armada had on the islands.

After Drake had foiled the invading Armada, the remnants of the crippled Spanish fleet were scattered into the North Sea. With the English vessels in pursuit, the Spanish Admiral of the Fleet ordered his ships to run for home, crossing the north of the British Isles, before limping homeward through the Atlantic.

But not all the Armada ships made it past the Northern Isles.

Writing in 1889, the Orkney antiquarian and folklorist, Walter Traill Dennison, of West Brough, Sanday, recorded the fate of some of these ships.

In a paper he wrote for the Orkney Natural History Society, he recited a number of oral traditions "gathered from the lips of old people."

Wrecked on the Fair Isle

Among these was the loss of the Armada flagship, *El Gran Grifon*, commanded by the Admiral, The Duke of Medina, which was wrecked on the Fair Isle, the island between Orkney and Shetland.

According to historian, Sir Robert Sibbald, the islanders had, at first, kindly entertained the crew but, as winter approached, they feared the extra population would quickly exhaust food supplies, causing everyone to starve.

But although the Spaniards have been paying well for all they received, a Fair Isle man, relating the tail to Traill Dennison, said: "Spanish money couldna' fill hungry bellies".

Accordingly, wrote Traill Dennison, the islanders threw any unfortunate Spaniard, found alone, over the cliffs. Then a quicker plan was devised the islanders deliberately collapsed the flagstone roof of the dwelling where Spaniards were sleeping.

The surviving Spaniards, including the Duke of Medina, then fled to Shetland. Here, the Duke enjoyed the hospitality of a Shetland laird who, it seems, later arranged his repatriation as far as Dunkirk.

Westray hospitality

However, if the hospitality of the Fair Isle's inhabitants left something to be desired, the folk of Westray more than compensated. Here, they were offered sanctuary, with a number not only settling on the island, but also marrying and beginning a unique community, vestiges of which survives today.

These Spanish settlers, and their descendants, became renowned as daring seafarers and notorious smugglers.

The Spanish seamen found themselves in Westray after a ship was wrecked in the fierce water of Dennis Rost, off North Ronaldsay. The surviving crewmen, who had taken to the lifeboats, then made their way to Westray looking for a safe place to make landfall.

The came ashore at Pierowall, thereafter, according to Traill Dennison, they:

"seem to have taken kindly to the island, where they built houses for themselves, married wives and formed a little settlement by themselves on what is called the North Shore.

"After the first union by marriage of the Spaniards with Orcadian females, none of the race were allowed to marry with any but the descendants of the original settlers, and their descendants have since been termed Dons.

"These Dons seem to have kept themselves strictly from intermarrying with the rest of the people for a time.

"The Dons seem to have adopted in most cases Orkney names. Among their principal names were Petrie, Reid and Hewison. Though their descendants in some cases can still be traced, the Dons, as a separate caste, no longer exist."

Traill Dennison's own grandfather, who lived at Noltland Castle, and who, in the summer months, traded with Continental ports, used to teach navigation and nautical skills to the young men of Westray.

He wrote: "During a pretty long life, he taught the nautical science to 140 young men, 80 per cent of whom are said to have been Dons."

"Most of these men left the county as sailors and many became sea captains," he added.

Apart from their proficiency as mariners, the Dons were also said to be fine actors who could entertain islanders with winter drama productions.

But although Traill Dennison had written that "the Dons, as a separate caste, no longer exist", he stressed that physical features remained that could still identify the descendants of the Armada survivors.

He wrote:

"The union of Spanish blood with the Norse produced a race of men active and daring; with dark eyes, and sometimes with features of a

foreign caste; in manners fidgety and restless a true Don being rarely able to sit in one position for five minutes, unless he was dead drunk; and in conversation more demonstrative and more given to gesticulate than the true Orcadian; while ready in wit, and perpetrating a practical joke, he was far superior to the native race."

The Seventeenth Century

The Covenanters and the Crown

In 1679, after the Scottish Covenanters' uprising was quashed at the Battle of Bothwell Brig, around 1,200 prisoners were herded into the open space at Greyfriar's Church in Edinburgh.

Many of these prisoners were set free after making submission, while some were executed and others died of illness, or wounds.

The 250 prisoners that were left proved a problem. They had to be "disposed" of somehow.

So, in November 1679, these unfortunates were lead on to a ship, the *Crown of London*, in Leith, where they were to be transported to English plantations in America to become slaves.

Under the command of one Captain Patterson, the *Crown of London* set sail in December 1679.

The captain's planned course is unknown, but the ship's first port of call was Orkney where, on December 10, 1679, she sheltered from a storm off Scarvataing, a headland in the parish of Deerness, a mile or two from the sheltered bay of Deer Sound.

In gales typical of the season, the ship was driven on to rocks after her anchor chain snapped. The captain and crew escaped the doomed vessel by hacking down the ship's mast and clambering across it to reach land.

The prisoners, however, were not so fortunate.

They had been confined to the hold and the hatches battened down under the captain's orders. The reasoning behind this act was simple the captain would be paid for the number of slaves on board the vessel and recompensed for those who died on the voyage. He would receive nothing for an escaped prisoner.

So, when the ship left port, Patterson took steps to make sure none did.

One member of crew did attempt a rescue by breaking through the deck with an axe. His valiant efforts meant that around 50 prisoners escaped and made it to the Deerness shore.

The remainder perished as the ship broke up and sank. It is said that over the following days, bodies washed up over three miles of the Deerness coastline.

Of the 47 or so prisoners who escaped to shore, most were recaptured and shipped to slavery in Jamaica, or New Jersey.

The people of Orkney were told that the prisoners were rebels fleeing from justice, but some are said to have escaped capture. Tradition has it that some survivors made it to Stromness, where they found passage on a ship to Holland. Local tradition also dictates that some were permitted to settle in Orkney.

It has also been suggested that the ship, filled with prisoners, was never meant to make it to the colonies. A fully-laden vessel, travelling the northern routes at that time of the year was bound to run into trouble, especially when it had no provisions adequate for such a major voyage.

At the time the Colonial ports in America were open only to ships from England a fact that makes it highly doubtful that a ship bearing cargo from Scotland would have been permitted to land.

Was there a darker motive behind the voyage of the *Crown of London*?

A monument for the Covenanters was erected in Deerness in 1888, three hundred yards from the spot where the ship went down.

Early Historical References to Orkney

The earliest surviving mention of the Orkney Islands is found in the accounts of the Roman geographer Diodorus Siculus.

Writing around 56BC, Diodorous set out to record an account of, what was then, the known world.

Diodorous's account is based on a report by the Greek sailor Pytheas of Massilia, who is thought to have sailed around Britain in 325 BC.

Pytheas' account of this journey, *Concerning the Ocean*, has since been lost, but his work was extensively quoted from over the following centuries.

Diodorus described Britain as triangular. The three points of this triangle, he wrote, were Cantium, Belerium and, jutting out into the open sea, Orkas - a place of immense waves.

"Britain is triangular in shape, much as is Sicily, but its sides are not equal. The island stretches obliquely along the coast of Europe, and the point where it is least distant from the continent, we are told, is the promontory which men call Kantion and thus is about one hundred stades from the mainland, at the place where the sea has its outlet, whereas the second promontory, known as Belerion, is said to be a voyage of four days from the mainland, and the last, writers tell us, extends out into the open sea and is named Orkas."

This promontory, Orkas or Orcas, is generally thought to be Dunnett Head in Caithness - the most northerly point of mainland Scotland. From here, Orkney is clearly visible across the Pentland Firth.

Orcades

By the first century AD, the islands were being referred to by their Latin name "Orcades" - the maps of the Roman geographer, Pomponius Mela, being the earliest surviving record of this name.

Later, around 98 AD, the Roman writer Tacitus, while documenting the campaigns of his father-in-law, the Roman general Agricola, states that after the defeat of the Picts at the battle of Mons Graupius, Agricola despatched a force to sail around the northern tip of Britain.

This expedition, which took place around 84AD, saw the explorers experience favourable weather and return unscathed after having first "discovered and subjugated the Orcades hitherto unknown".

According to Tacitus, these islands were "beaten by a wild and open sea".

He then goes on to tell how the explorers sighted the island of Thule before being forced southwards by the onset of winter.

The position of Thule has been long debated but it is generally thought that the Roman seamen sighted Shetland. Some scholars believe Agricola actually reached and landed in Shetland.

People, Culture and Tradition
Tradition

Orcadian Customs and Traditions

Life in the Orkney islands is, and always has been, steeped in tradition.

These days, some of these customs remain strong while others have become mere shadows of their former selves if not forgotten altogether.

As with our folklore, the islands' various traditions revolved around the realities and demands of island life the elements, work, the cyclical pattern of the seasons and the inevitable cycle of life birth, marriage and death.

As is always the case, these traditions are dying out rapidly as the old folk, the last guardians, slip away, one by one taking the unwritten wealth with them to the grave.

Annual Festivities

The Festival of the Horse and Boys' Ploughing Match

Once a year, in the island of South Ronaldsay, mothers and fathers delve deep into their attics and cupboards.

They are preparing for a tradition believed to be unique to Orkney which dates back to at least the early 19th century.

Metal ploughs are polished, buttons are cleaned, ribbons replaced and the youngsters are ready to go. Ahead of them is a very important date in the South Ronaldsay calendar the South Ronaldsay Boys' Ploughing Match and the Festival of the Horse.

Although the earliest records of the event come from the 1800s, but it is not known exactly when the tradition began.

Originally, only young boys had participated, either in the ploughing or being dressed as the horse (mimicking the Clydesdale horse decoration), but following a revival in the 20th century, it was decided girls could take part, but only as horses.

In the early days the ploughing was done in a 'Hope kailyard. These days the activity has moved to the beach at the Sands o' Wright.

The early ploughs often just consisted of an ox hoof, or horn, tied to a stick. In 1920, the first miniature metal plough was made by the local blacksmith, Bill Hourston. Some of these are still in use today, and they are works of art, being precise replicas in every detail of full-size adult ploughs.

In the competition, each furrow must be identical to its neighbour. With a four to five feet square patch, the boys must plough straight and even furrows over the whole area.

The judges look for the best start, which includes how the boys set the dreels, and the neatest ending of their work, as well as the overall ploughing. No help is allowed when ploughing. The fathers, grandfathers and uncles can only stand back and watch and hope their painstaking tuition has paid off.

The "horse" outfits, are spectacular. A collar, hat, belt and feet decorations are added to complete the overall picture. A tail can be fixed to the jacket and pom-poms or fringes sewn on the cuffs to resemble the forefeet.

The Kirkwall Ba'

Every Christmas Eve and Hogmanay, householders and shopkeepers along Kirkwall's winding central streets can be seen barricading doors and windows in preparation for the following days' ba' games.

The Kirkwall Ba' is a mass-football game played out in the streets of the town every Christmas Day and New Year's Day.

The game pits two rival "factions" against each other in a battle to secure a goal and win the game.

Uppies and Doonies

The men and boys of Kirkwall are designated either "Uppies" or "Doonies", or "Up the Gates" and "Doon the Gates". This is thought to be a corruption of the Old Norse *gata*, meaning *road*.

Whether you were an Uppie or a Doonie originally depended upon the individual's place of birth. Those born to the north of the Cathedral were a Doonies, with Uppies being those born to the south.

These days, however, family loyalty is usually more important than the place of birth, with stalwart players playing for the same side as their father, grandfathers and great-grandfathers did before them, regardless of where they now live.

The ba'

The ba' itself is a handmade, cork-filled, leather ball. Each game is played with a new ba', each one handmade by one of a few Orcadian ba' makers.

A finished Men's ba' weighs about 3 lbs with a circumference of approximately 28 inches. The Boys' Ba' is slightly smaller.

The ba' shown right was won by my grandfather, George Borwick, in the 1950 Christmas Day game. This ba' is now well over 100 years old, having first been used in 1898.

The game begins

Two ba' games are played every Christmas and New Year's Day.

The first, the Boys' Ba', begins at 10.30am. If the battle for the Boys' Ba' is long and hard, it is not uncommon for it, and the Men's Ba', which starts at 1pm, to be running concurrently.

The game begins on Kirkwall's Broad Street, in the shadow of St Magnus Cathedral.

The Uppie goal is to touch the ba' against a wall in the south end of the town, while the Doonies have the unenviable task of getting the ba' into the water of Kirkwall Bay, to the north.

There are no hard and fast rules. Although the game is fairly rough, tempers are usually held in check and foul play, or "inappropriate behaviour", is not tolerated. Surprisingly, given the nature of the Ba', serious injuries to players are fairly rare. More often than not it is usually unfamiliar spectators who are hurt. When the pack breaks, there is often not much room to run!

As the cathedral clock strikes 1pm, a specially chosen individual, usually someone with a long association with the game, throws the ba' from the Mercat Cross into the gathered crowd of players. As soon as it lands in the pack, the fight for possession begins, with each side trying to gain ground and carry the ba' towards their territories.

A tight scrum forms around the leather trophy, while players on the outside brace themselves against any nearby buildings to prevent the opposition capturing ground. With the streets now their playing field, a heaving throng of men push and pulling to try and gain a few metres nearer their goal. In the cold, winter air, steam hangs above the pack.

But when the pack breaks, chaos erupts, as those in possession of the ba' try and get as close to their goal as possible before being stopped. As soon as they are intercepted, however, the scrum quickly reforms.

This struggle to gain ground means that a typical game can last for hours. Based on recent years, an average Men's Ba' lasts about five hours, but this could be anything up to eight hours, or more.

Throughout the game, numerous tactics are used to achieve the goal. Very often, the majority of players have no idea where the ba' actually is. This leads to numerous attempts to smuggle the ba' out of the pack or create fake "breaks" in the hope that the opposition will follow the wrong players.

A successful break allows players to sprint towards their goal, making the most of Kirkwall's winding lanes to slow down pursuers. Players have been known to attempt to reach their goals via the rooftops.

When the goal is finally reached, the ba' itself a coveted trophy is awarded to a player in the winning side who has been a notable participant over a number of years.

> "It breaks out twice a year at a time when peace and goodwill might be expected to prevail, the warring armies engaging in close combat with a ferocity that precludes respect for person or property.
>
> "Even the law has been known to stand impotent as combatants surged and counter-surged through the environs of the police station, and memory has hardly dimmed the occasion when the local manse was invaded and despoiled. Casualties are high but who cares?
>
> "Crushed ribs and broken limbs are never enough reasons for the enthusiastic participants to desist from this traditional orgy of Orcadian violence which not even a sheriff's edict could ban the Kirkwall Ba' Game."

Yule The Midwinter Festival

From the dawn of time, the need to celebrate the winter solstice, and the subsequent 'rebirth' of the sun, was an absolute necessity.

An Orkney winter is long, cold and dark. It is a bleak time, when the weak, grey sun barely crawls above the horizon for a few hours each day.

Life goes on, but mostly in darkness.

Even today, the winter solstice remains significant to Orcadians, although, in most cases, subconsciously. Once the shortest day has passed, and although we know that the worst of the winter may yet come, it is comforting to know that the days are lengthening, once again, and that the light is returning.

The return of the light

By the winter solstice the shortest day of year the sun rises in Orkney well after 9am and is beginning to set again by 2pm. Assuming clear conditions, this leaves a mere six hours of weak daylight.

But the solstice marks a turning point.

The darkness has reached its zenith and soon the days will lengthen again. In this, the darkest time of the year, what better way to celebrate the return of light, and warmth, than to feast and make merry.

The midwinter traditions surrounding the festival of Yule were once strong in Orkney. So much so that even in the early years of the 20th century, in the more remote corners of the islands, the winter festivities were still referred to as Yule. It was rare indeed to hear folk speak of "Christmas".

Like the other festivals of the year, Yule was a great social occasion, relieving, if only for a brief time, the hardship and monotony of the islanders' subsistence living.

But Yule was not only about celebrating the return of the light...

The dead return...

Being the darkest time of the year, midwinter, and Yule in particular, was also a time when supernatural forces were able to cross to the realm of man, and the spirits of the dead would return to their families.

As such, most of the Yule customs we remember today were originally to protect the household against these paranormal influences.

Over the years, the pagan Yule traditions were overlaid with elements of Christianity, but, as is common in the islands, old traditions die-hard and some of the ancient customs persisted until the early 19th century.

Unfortunately, however, these are now all but forgotten, as practically no Orcadian Yule customs were recorded by early scholars.

But all is not lost.

We can at least get an inkling of what went on by referring to the documented customs found in Shetland, where the traditions of Yule were more extensively collected and documented.

Orkney's Harvest Lore

The Orkney Islands have a long and illustrious farming history.

At one time, the islands' golden swathes of crop fields were renowned across Europe, so much so that a mid-sixteenth century account described Orkney as:

"The chief nourishers and storers of the southland with Corne, victell and oil."

The people of Orkney have worked the land for millennia, and, until the 19th century, there was very little change in the tools or methods used.

Considering the length of time the islands' fertile soils have been worked, it will come as no surprise to learn that many of our most tenacious traditions were firmly rooted in the earth. As such, many ancient customs surrounded the everyday tasks carried out in the fields.

In these days of supermarkets and intensive farming techniques, it's all too easy to forget that, to my forebears, a poor harvest meant a harsh winter with starvation and, very possibly, death.

Is it any wonder that many of their customs were to ensure fertile fields and a bounteous "hairst", or harvest.

Traditionally, the high point of the agricultural year was the successful gathering and storing of the harvest, but in Orkney's agricultural past there were many customs that had to be observed before these final celebrations.

Gyro Night

The Night of the Ogress

An interesting old tradition, once celebrated every February on the island of Papay went by the name of "Gyro Night". The last occurrence of Gyro Night, however, was in 1914 and it is now but a memory.

The actual date of Gyro Night is not found in any surviving account, but one reference indicates that the ceremony took place after the first full moon in February.

This date connects the tradition with the Christian festival of Candlemas, as well as the Celtic celebration of Imbolc, an event marking the end of winter and the beginning of spring.

Boyish games

Although we are not certain of the date, we do know that, on Gyro Night, the young boys of the island made torches, which they set alight, before venturing out into the night.

The purpose of their foray was to entice the "gyros" out of hiding.

These gyros were usually the older lads, wearing masks and dressed as repulsive old women. If the torchbearers met a gyro, "she" would pursue the youngsters, striking at them with a piece of rope, or tangle, until they were able to outrun "her".

The origin of this tradition is unclear, but it is likely that *gyro* derives from the Norse, *gygr,* meaning a giant, troll-woman.

But what was the significance of this monstrous woman?

The key lies in an account that refers to the burning of a female effigy on Gyro Night. This adds weight to the theory that Gyro Night was connected to Imbolc, the Celtic celebration of winter's end.

The winter hag and the reborn goddess

The fact that the tradition is only recorded as taking place in Papay is particularly interesting, given the island's association with early Christianity.

Imbolc was linked to the pagan Celtic goddess Brigid and, in keeping with the policy of the early church to absorb pagan festivals into Christian feast-days, Brigid, became St Bride.

St Bride's Day became equated with Candlemas on February 2 the feast of the Purification of the Blessed Virgin Mary. So, the fires that were an integral part of the pagan festival in particular the torchlight processions leading to a bonfire were tamed down, with candles replacing the burning brands.

Looking to Celtic tradition, we can begin to see information that appears to shed light on Papay's Gyro Night.

For example, in the Scottish Highlands, and Ireland, an effigy of the spirit of winter â€" the Cailleach, or Old Wife â€" was burned on a bonfire. This wizened crone was thought to be reborn, at Imbolc, in the form of the goddess Brigid.

Did the later Norse inhabitants of Papay incorporate these existing traditions, interpreting the old woman of winter as the ogress-like Gygr? The presence of traditions surrounding Brigid/Bride are also borne out by the occurrence of 'Bride' placenames in Papay.

But what of the connection to the Norse ogress? For that we need to look at the Celtic idea that the reborn goddess emerged from a burial mound.

A Scottish rhyme about the Feast Day of Bride begins:

This is the day of Bride,
The queen will come from the mound...

To the Norse Orcadians, the usual inhabitant of burial mounds was the monstrous creature known as the draugr.

Over the centuries, the draugr beliefs degenerated into those of the trows and hogboon, but original fragments of lore hint that the mound's original inhabitant could often be found with his mother a beast said to be even more terrible than her son.

So do we have a situation where the islanders equated the Celtic hag in the mound with their ideas of a monstrous ogress dwelling in the howe? And was this the reason the Celtic night of the Goddess became equated with the Scandinavian gygr?

Given the lack of other information about this lost tradition, speculation is all we have left.

Orcadian Bonfire Traditions

The sky was a vivid crimson in every airt. Great bonfires flamed and the bairns were delirious with delight."

In the words of an old Orcadian author: "bonfires are the very blood of Orcadians. The ritual bonfire goes back to the very beginnings of our history and even before."

A perfect description.

Orkney is a place where absolute dark reigns for half the year. So the ceremonial lighting up of the night sky with fire was an eagerly awaited occasion.

In days gone by, four times every year, hilltops across Orkney blazed with orange firelight.

Giant bonfires were constructed and lit to commemorate the ancient festivals of Yule, Beltane, Johnsmas (midsummer) and Hallowmas (Halloween).

Over time, the tradition of lighting bonfires at Yule and Beltane died out. The third altered slightly, with the Hallowmas bonfires becoming associated with the national celebration of Guy Fawkes' Night, and therefore being lit around November 5.

Johnsmas was the last of the festivals widely celebrated with bonfires. The lighting midsummer bonfires remained in most Orkney toonships until the 1860s.

Preparing the fire

The responsibility for finding and gathering the material for the festival bonfires fell on the older children of each area. Because wood was far too scarce a commodity to waste in a fire, the main sources of fuel were heather and peat.

So, in the weeks leading up to the fire, the youngsters of the community would wander the hills, gathering armfuls of heather. These would be carted back and stored near the bonfire site. Every house in the area also permitted the gatherers to take as many peats from their stack as the strongest boy could carry away.

The site of the bonfires was usually a traditional one a place where the celebratory fires had been lit for countless generations. The massive cliff in Hoy, St John's Head, is so called because it was the site of the Johnsmas bonfires from time immemorial.

Fireside antics

When the night of the fire finally arrived and the bonfire was ablaze, the youngsters danced and capered around the flames. The boys would pull burning bits of heather from the fire and run across the hillsides, setting them alight! Antics such as jumping through the flames were normal and generally expected.

Early records from the seventeenth century tell us that those who gathered to watch the bonfire's leaping flames would walk around its circumference "with the sun" in other words, clockwise. In much the same way, cattle, horses, the sick or infirm were also led sunwise around the fire. The bonfire's flames were regarded as having some form of purifying or revitalising power.

The importance placed on the power of flame remained until the middle of the nineteenth century. Until this time, farmers throughout the county carried torches of blazing heather around their fields, through their byres and among their cattle in the belief that this would make them thrive. In much the same manner there are also records of houses being circled with torches of burning heather.

The power of fire was also thought to protect against the powers of evil in whatever shape or form they stalked the land.

A Year of Orcadian Tradition

"The Aurora dances in the north like a princess or a tinker lass," says January. "A bird starves here and there."

January

The first day of the New Year was commonly marked by mass ball games, none of which now survive, except the New Year's Ba' in Kirkwall.

A New Year tradition, once common in Orkney and Shetland, was the singing of the "Neuer Sang" (New Year Song). This song would appear to be of medieval origin and was, at some point, imported into the islands from mainland Scotland.

Thereafter, the song became a firm part of island tradition and was sung at New Year by wandering bands of young men, who visited each house in their district. The singers were rewarded for their efforts with food and ale.

One of the band was referred to as the "Kyerrin Horse" and this individual was equipped with a straw basket into which the householders deposited "gifts".

Up until World War One, New Year's Day was observed according to the Julian Calendar known in the islands as the "old calendar"

January 13 was therefore known as "Aald Neuerday", a tradition maintained in some of the islands longer than others.

February

"I wear grey patches of snow on my drab coat," says February.
"But I have a few snowdrops in my hand."

One interesting old tradition once celebrated in February took place on the island of Papay. The actual date in February of the celebration of "Gyro Night" is not recorded, but on that night we know that the young boys would venture out into the darkness hunting for "gyros" The origin of this tradition is uncertain although it is certain that "gyro" derives from the Norse "gygr" a giant, troll-woman.

March

"I weigh day and night" says March, the shopkeeper.
"There you are sir a shillingworth of sun."

In Orkney, March is the month of lengthening days and the spring equinox. The long dark winter is behind us and a summer of long days and darkling twilights lies ahead.

March sees the "Vore Tullye" the spring struggle between the evil Teran and the Mither o' the Sea.

During this time, the islands are battered by incessant winds and storms, said to be the result of the violent clash between these ancient spirits of winter and summer.

April

"Who brings lambs and first daffodils?
April and she lights a score of hill fires."

April 1 was known as "Gokky Day" (Fool's Day) or "Gokky Hunt" (Hunt the Fool) and was celebrated in much the same way as "All Fool's Day" with practical jokes and tricks played on the unwary.

April 2 "Tailing Day"; On Tailing Day Orcadian children would secretly pin "tails" to each other while the more daring would target teachers and other "upstanding" adults.

More recently, the tails were made from paper, or cord, but there was a time when local butchers would save pigs' tails, which were then attached to the unsuspecting, with bent pins.

The tradition is practically dead these days, although it was one we still took part in as children.

April 3 "Borrowing Day"; A rather strange custom, but anything borrowed on this day became the immediate property of the borrower.

This tradition lingered on in Orkney until the 1930s.

April 16 St Magnus Day Mansmas the feast day of Orkney's most revered saint.

Easter In the islands, the term "Easter" was not used until the middle of the 1900s.

However the festival was celebrated. Children were given eggs and encouraged to eat as many as possible.

In South Ronaldsay a unique Easter custom took place in which the local boys competed in a ploughing match, using beautifully-made miniature ploughs, more often than not family heirlooms.

At the same time, the girls and boys sometimes of the island dressed up in ornately crafted, and colourful, symbolic "horse" costumes. The "Festival of the Horse" now takes place later in the year primarily, I believe, to cater for visiting tourists.

May

"May herds the cuithes in legions through the Sound.

There are no recorded Orcadian traditions surrounding the ancient festival of Beltane, although we do know that at one time bonfires were lit at Beltane, as well as Yule, Midsummer and Hallowmas.

Gradually the bonfire festivals at Yule, Beltane and Midsummer died out, leaving only the Hallowmas bonfires (November 1). For more information on Orkney's bonfire traditions. The wild weather sometimes experienced around Beltane was referred to as the "Beltane Tirls" a fact that certainly indicates that the festival was acknowledged at one time.

In Orkney, animals born around Beltane in particular cats were expected to be poor, sickly creatures. It was therefore said to be unlucky to set a hen "between the Beltanes" as the chicks would be "noatheen bit a lok o' June yappicks".

(The term "between the Beltanes" referred to the difference between the old Julian calendar and the later Gregorian system.)

As in other parts of Britain, the tradition of washing your face in the Mayday dew was common. Youngsters would, and perhaps still do, climb to the top of notable hills to carry out this ritual. See June for more on this subject.

Up until World War One, May was the month when Orcadian children had their winter boots taken from them. They would then run barefoot, regardless of the weather, until after the harvest was brought in.

As is mentioned in the Wedding Traditions section, for some unknown, superstitious, reason, the month of May was always avoided for weddings.

The folklorist Ernest Marwick claimed that this was due to the month's association with the Roman festival of the dead, although I can't quite see what relevance this would have had to the people of Orkney.

June

"June hardly sleeps. Hardly has she covered the fire in the North-West than it's time to kindle the fire in the north-east.
She spreads beautiful cloths everywhere, stitched with flowers."

June is the lightest month in the Orkney calendar. As the sun climbs to its zenith, at the summer solstice, it barely dips below the western horizon. At this time of the year, it is quite possible to read outside at midnight I can personally vouch for this, having done it a few times myself.

The midsummer festivities are the most prominent in this month.

Up until the middle of the 19th century, Midsummer, or Johnsmas, bonfires were lit on hills across the islands. For more information on the island's bonfire traditions.

The young people from Stromness and Sandwick used to climb to the summit of the hill, Kringlafiold, for three mornings, at midsummer, to meet the rising sun with outstretched arms.

One account of this ritual has the young folk kissing the palms of their hands before uplifting them to the newly risen sun. I wonder whether this tradition may has any connection to the fact that the name Kringlafiold meaning "round hill" could refer to a natural spring found on the hill.

Given the multitude of Celtic traditions surrounding similar sacred springs and wells, was the face washing ritual connected to the hallowed waters of the spring?

According to some, the selkies, who were condemned to wander through the seas until the Day of Judgement, were permitted to shed their sealskins and assume human form on Johnsmas Eve.

July

"July is a riot of schoolchildren. And a doucer riot of tourists, saying, "How quaint!"
Fields are scored with green and yellow geometry."

In bygone days, there was no time in July for festivals.
Although the the long days, and nights of perpetual twilight, had descended on the islands, winter was rapidly approaching. Chores needed doing. Fish had to be caught and dried for the winter. Peats were cut, spread, brought in and stacked an onerous task, believe me I had to do it as a boy and other work around the farm or croft carried out.

It is therefore not surprising that there are no recorded traditions in Orkney surrounding the month of July.

Despite this, as always we can turn our heads further north to the Shetland islands where a date observed as "Martin o' Balymas Day" was observed.
This day, July 4, was also celebrated to the south of Orkney, in Caithness, but here it was known as "St Bulgan's Day". As these dates exist in the areas immediately surrounding Orkney, it is fairly certain that we can assume the occasion was once marked by Orcadians also.

The names of the day used in Shetland and Caithness is a corruption of "St Martin of Bullion's Day" which is in turn a mispronunciation of "Martin le Bouillant".
In the Northern Isles, this feast day took over the day traditionally ascribed to St Swithin and was said to mark the beginning of six weeks

of dry weather. If the feast was greeted by a gale of wind, however, as is unfortunately all too common, rain would be sure to follow.

August

"'Well", says August, "time to gather all the riches together in a field full of folk."

August was the month in which the greatest Orkney holiday of the year was held the Lammas Market. Lammas, also called "Lughnasad", was an ancient celebration of the first harvest, and honoured the grain harvests, as well as the gods and goddesses of death and resurrection.

Lughnasadh meaning "festival of Lugh" or Lammas meaning "festival of the loaves" ("hlaf-mass") fell on August 1. In Kirkwall, the Lammas Market took place over 11 days, and was proclaimed through the streets of the town by the town officer, preceded by a drummer. These days, however, the Lammas Fair is forgotten. In its heyday, the Lammas Fair attracted folk from across the islands, who all headed into the town to be entertained by showmen, tricksters and entertainers.

To cope with the incredible influx of visitors, poor, but adequate, accommodation was offered throughout Kirkwall. These Lammas "beuls" were, very often, just a straw-covered floors on which the visiting islanders rested, in the company of a number of strangers.

An interesting tradition surrounding the fair is that the young men were advised to place a four-leafed clover in their boots. This was believed to give them the power to see through the tricks employed by the visiting cheap-jacks. Examples of the reliability of this charm are actually recorded. One story relates that a crowd, gathered around a Lammas booth to watch a dancing cockerel, were asked by an old woman why they were so interested in a bird with straws fixed to its legs. It was only then that the sheepish onlookers realised that they had been mesmerised by the crafty showman.

The old woman was immune to his tricks because there was a four-leaved clover hidden within the grass she carried.

September

"I measure night and day," says September the joiner.
"Not long now, at the longest, the dark."

September was, and still is, the month of harvest. Many of the traditions surrounding harvest are now forgotten but, at one time, this was the busiest, and most laborious, period of the Orkney farming year. For full details of old Orcadian harvest lore.

The Feast of St Michael, Michaelmas, was celebrated in the islands on September 29 October 12, by the Old Style calendar. It has been suggested that Orkney's "Muckle Feast" is actually a corruption of the "Mikkel Feast" "Mikkel" being the Norse for "Michael"..

September sees the arrival of the "Gore Vellye" the Autumn Tumult a time when equinoctial gales batter the islands. The early Orcadians explained these weather conditions as the result of a fearsome battle between the Sea Mither and her bitter nemesis, Teran.

October

"In my house," says October, "there are witches.
There are apples and nuts."
Then October again, offering a child an apple in the door. And if you go in, she'll tell you a story of witchcraft at her fire.

The start of the long northern winter is now completely upon us. The long summer twilights are replaced by cold, empty nights of total darkness. It is therefore not surprising that, in days past, preparation for the rapidly approaching winter were well under way by October.

The third Sunday of the month was once referred to as "Winter Sunday Fastening". This was the day that the cattle, who had roamed free all summer, were brought in from the fields and confined to the byre for the winter.

Even today, seeing the "kye" move to byre is a solemn occassion a realisation that the darkness of winter awaits.

In Orkney, October is most renowned for the ancient festival of the dead Hallowe'en. Like the rest of Britain, Orkney celebrates the festival in practically the same way. Lanterns are carved from turnips and great care taken to avoid the influences of the dead. The lanterns, referred to as "Neepy Lanterns", are carried from house to house where each householder gives the bearer "a penny for the lantern".

In Stromness, the carved turnip takes a different slant. There, the children carve heads from turnips and after impaling them on sticks go from door to door asking for a "Penny for me Pop".

This is all that remains of an older anti-Catholic tradition where the townsfolk asked for a "penny to burn the Pope".

Until recently, Halloween was more commonly referred to as "Devilment Night" in recognition of the pranks carried out by the youngsters on this night. Generally a blind eye was turned on the youngsters exploits pranks had been carried out for generations.

The "devilment" dialect term for "mischief" continues strong to this day with unwary travellers often finding themselves falling victim to showers of egg, flour, treacle and foam.

At one time, Halloween was regarded as the best night in which to attempt to divine the future, particularly relating to matters of the heart.

November

"'I keep the bones of the dead,' says November.
"But a bright one, a saint, looks out the window, and a candle is burning."

By November, winter's cloak of darkness has well and truly settled over the islands, with perhaps only six hours of weak, grey sunlight between sunrise and sunset.

Hallowmas November 1 was one of the four occasions in Orkney celebrated by lighting bonfires. The Hallowmas bonfires continued well after the midsummer and Beltane fires had died out. To a certain extent the Hallowmas bonfires continue to this day although they have long since been incorporated into the Guy Fawkes celebrations.

November was often referred as the "month of the dead". Because of the worsening winter conditions, it was often thought that November was the time the old folk passed away.

December

"I have hundreds of candles," says December.
"Was ever such intricate jewellery as the first snowflake?
There's an inn, a crib, an ox and an ass."

December is the month of the winter solstice, an event recognised by the ancient Orcadians and commemorated within the Neolithic chamber of Maeshowe.

There, the setting sun is aligned with the entrance of the tomb and, as it disappears beneath the horizon, the last dying rays strike the rear of the ancient chamber.

December was also the month of the festival of Yule, a time at which the hordes of trows were at their most menacing. Compared with Shetland, very few Orcadian Yule traditions are remembered, or were recorded, but it is generally agreed that the festival lasted most of December, possibly beginning on December 12. Like all the major seasonal festivals, Yule was at one time marked by the lighting of ceremonial bonfires.

A common Yule observance was that "A green Yule means a full kirkyard". Although this saying is now rarely heard, there is still a firm belief in the principle behind it. Spates of illness throughout the year are often blamed on the fact that there was no snow the previous winter.

On Christmas morning, the men of Kirkwall participate in the Ba' a mass football game between the two sides of the town the "uppies", from the south end and the "doonies", from the north.

Along the same lines as the Ba', in Stromness, Christmas Eve was marked by a symbolic tug-of-war style game in which a tree a rarity in Orkney was stolen from a garden and bound and chained in the middle of the town's long street.

The men from the north of the town then fought the south-enders for the tree, each side attempting to drag it to a goal well within their own territory.

Charms and Healing

Holy Wells and Magical Waters

"Wherever there was a spring, the was life; wherever there was life, there was a spirit"

Fresh water is one of life's basic necessities. Without it nothing can thrive.

It is little wonder, therefore, that from prehistoric times, fresh water has been regarded as a precious substance. These days, the act of being able to turn a tap has led us to take water for granted.

In Orkney, until the advent of piped water in the 20th century, water for croft and household was drawn from the hundreds of wells dotted across the islands.

Although in latter years, many of these wells were simply regarded as sources of water, others retained a special significance a significance that could well hark back to prehistoric tradition and ritual.

A number of wells, and springs, were regarded as particularly special, even magical, especially if they were some distance away from an existing watercourse. In ancient times, places where the life-giving water trickled from a hillside, or welled up from the earth, must surely have been regarded as a gift from the gods.

But it was not only its practical requirements for sustaining life that made water significant to the early people of Orkney.

In Iron Age ritual, for example, bodies of water were regarded as a gateway between worlds a barrier between the natural world and the supernatural.

Consequently, springs and wells were frequently thought to be the dwelling places of the gods, or entrances to the Otherworld. Because of this they were often the repositories of Iron Age artefacts with items cast into the water as votive offerings.

Elements of these ancient beliefs persisted through the millennia, and were incorporated into the traditions and customs surrounding Orkney's many holy wells.

These wells were thought to possess magical properties offering, for example, the powers of healing, or divination.

With the advent of Christianity, the church tried to eradicate these "pagan" practices but found the veneration of wells very difficult to eradicate

> "no one shall go to trees, or wells, or stones or enclosures, or anywhere else except to God's church, and there make vows or release himself from them."

The Penitentials of Theodoris. 7th century AD.

Around 640 AD, St Eligius ordered that:

"no Christian place lights at the temples or at the stones, or at fountains and springs, or at trees, or at places where three ways meet. .. Let no one presume to purify by sacrifice, or to enchant herbs, or to make flocks pass through a hollow tree or an aperture in the earth; for by so doing he seems to consecrate them to the devil."

These efforts, however, were in vain, so, in Orkney, as elsewhere, the Church changed tactics. Instead, it tried to absorb pagan traditions rather than eradicate them completely.

As the pagan and Christian practices blended together, the wells gradually became holy wells. Where once they were the haunt of spirits and fairies, they became associated with the cult of a local saint, local monks or even the cleaning of sacred vessels.

The wells remained the places of pilgrimage and worship, but the objects of veneration became Christian motifs, that usually incorporated pagan elements of the original.

A prime example of the Christian "adoption" of a holy well is Manswal St Magnus Well in Birsay.

The water of this well was thought to be highly medicinal, not only because the holy remains of St Magnus were said to have rested there but also, according to some local variants of the tale, the saint's bones were actually washed in the waters.

But just as water was a source of life, as any islander will know, it is also dangerous and able to take life and destroy. And just as wells or springs were usually regarded as beneficial, there were cases where they were tainted by an air of evil and shunned. Few of these "evil" wells still exist, or their whereabouts recorded.

It may be that some of these "evil" wells were simply polluted or foul perhaps responsible for the death of livestock or people and this may be the reason behind their reputation.

For the others there are a number of possibilities.

The spread of Christianity may hold the key to some. Did the church declare some of the more tenacious customs surrounding "water-worship" blasphemous, and the site demonised, by the clergy?

Alternatively, the fear and awe surrounding some wells may hark back to the ancient beliefs that they were Otherworldly doors a gateway that allowed supernatural denizens to access to our world. The number of sites linked with fairies or trows in later years, such as Keldereddie and Fursokelda in Birsay, would seem to confirm this.

Naturally, the fact that some wells were renowned haunts of trows and fairies was enough for any superstitious Orcadian of yesteryear to shun them.

It is also possible that some of the beneficent wells we know today were once looked upon with dread.

We know from accounts elsewhere, that the church blessed the waters of "unholy" wells in an effort to remove the superstitious fear and their associations with heathen practices.

Dian-stanes and "Thunderstones"

Just as the possession of an elf-arrow, or elf-dart, was once thought to protect against the fairy-folk, acquiring a "dian-stane" was a sure means of gaining protection from the malicious influences of the trows.

However, within our surviving folklore, the distinction between the elf-arrow and the dian-stane has blurred. In some cases the object known as an elf-arrow usually a prehistoric flint arrowhead, axe or knife has also come to be referred to as a dian-stane.

The thunderstone divine protector

For the origin of Orkney's dian-stane traditions we must turn to the root of the name itself, which is simply a corruption of the Norse term *dynestein*, meaning *thunderstone*.

These thunderstones are found throughout Scandinavian folklore and tradition. They were generally quartz, or quartz-like, stones, pebbles, crystals or even flints usually uncovered in fields when ploughing.

The dynesteins were thought to fall from the sky during thunderstorms missiles hurled by the pagan god Thor to to keep the wandering trolls under control. If a thunderstone struck a troll foolish enough to be out in a thunderstorm, instant death followed.

According to Norwegian folklore, were it not for Thor's missiles, the trolls would have spread across the earth like a plague.

The Orcadian version of the these thunderstones inevitably offered protection against trows loosely an Orcadian variant of the troll and so it was common for them to be built into the walls of houses or outbuildings.

Incorporating a dian-stane into a building not only ensured that the trows left a farmstead alone, but was also thought to protect the structure from lightning.

This protection from lightning is also recorded in Switzerland. There, during a storm, the thunderstone was tied to string and swung three times around the owner's head before being thrown at the door of his house.

Luckystones shadows of their former selves

Over time, these powerful charmed stones became regarded as nothing more than lucky talismans.

As the centuries passed, the potency of the dian-stanes decreased until, by the time of my childhood, they were simply referred to as "luckystones" or "luck stones".

To carry such a pebble was thought to bring the bearer good luck but only after spitting on them and polishing the surface. As a boy, numerous "luckystones" lay throughout the house, carried indoors whenever we found one.

The holed talisman a sun symbol?

Inextricably tied up with the lore of the thunderstones are the ancient customs involving a separate class of protective stone those that were holed or perforated.

In a paper describing old Orkney farming customs, the writer Ernest Marwick had no doubts that the dian-stane was round, flat and holed. These holed stones were an integral part of spring's most important task ploughing the fields.

Before the introduction of the mechanical tractor, the dian-stane was strung, with strands of horsehair, from the body of the horse or ox-drawn plough.

Then, while ploughing, the ploughman ensured that at the end of each furrow, when he turned to start another, the stone was moved to the other side of the plough. This ensured the stone always faced the sun.

Once ploughing was complete, the dian-stane was hung from a nail in the dwellinghouse always in a position that ensured it was bathed in sunlight.

The reasoning behind this tradition is not certain but Ernest Marwick was convinced that the round stone represented the sun and symbolically ensured warmth returned to the cold earth.

Is was also known for the crofter to use the dian-stane when venturing to sea on fishing trips. In these cases, the stone was taken from its resting place and worn around the neck.

From accounts detailing customs surrounding these other holed stones, there is perhaps another common link the horse. For some reason the holed stones were thought to be particularly effective at protecting horses and therefore hung in or outside stables.

Although we have no surviving records connecting dian-stanes directly or exclusively to horses, there seems to have been a definite link. As we have seen, the stone had to be fastened to the plough with strands of horsehair.

The Charm of the 'Wreestin' Threed'

An intriguing piece of Orcadian folk magic was known as the "Wreestin' Threed" the wristing, or wresting, thread.

Used as a cure for sprains, the charm required a verse to be recited each time one of nine, equally spaced, knots were tied in a piece of thread. The verse went:

Oor Savior rade,
His fore-foot slade;
Our Savior lichtit down.
Sinew to sinew, vein to vein,
Joint to joint, and bane to bane,
Mend thoo in Geud's name!

What is particularly interesting about this charm, is that it appears to be a survival, or variant, of a pre-Christian charm also found in pagan Germany.

The charm, part of the Merseburg Incantations, was used by the Norse god Odin to heal the god Balder's horse:

Phol and Wodan rode into the woods,
There Balder's foal sprained its foot.
It was charmed by Sinthgunt, her sister Sunna;
It was charmed by Frija, her sister Volla;
It was charmed by Wodan, as he well knew how:
Bone-sprain, like blood-sprain,
Like limb-sprain:
Bone to bone; blood to blood;
Limb to limb -like they were glued.

Language and Custom

About the Orkney Islands

The Orcadian dialect

"The chief peculiarity of the Orkney dialect is its accentuation, the intonations of the voice, long marked by abrupt rises and falls so as to form a sort of cadence."

For 950 years from approximately AD800 until the middle of the 1700s the spoken language in Orkney was a variant of Old Norse known as Norrœna, or Norn.

Remnants of this now extinct language can still be clearly heard in today's Orcadian dialect a dialect shot through with Norse words and turns of speech.

Unfortunately, however, Orkney's dialect is at a low ebb changing rapidly due to the constant influences of television and education as well as the large number of incomers now settled in the islands.

These days, many placename pronunciations bear no resemblance to what they should be, words have been forgotten and names changed.

In years past, to speak with an Orcadian accent was regarded as a mark of ignorance. So, like many altered cultures across the planet, the natives were forced to change to suit to settlers.

Fortunately the days are gone in which the dialect was deliberately suppressed in schools although not that long gone. This practise was still the case in my schooldays.

But all is not lost. There have been efforts to revitalise the dialect and thanks to the efforts of some, Orkney's dialect is no longer something that is regarded as the "speech of the ignorant". Our local radio presenters often use dialect not without the protest of some and there are now books documenting the vanishing language. In addition, a growing number of Orcadian writers also utilise it in their work.

As long as we remember that over one thousand years of tradition and heritage went into the 'language' of the islands, and that the past thirty years has seen the destruction of so much, then perhaps the Orkney Norn can survive long into the 21st century.

> "The men spoke for the most part in a slow deliberate voice, but some of the women could rattle on at a great rate in the soft sing-song lilt of the islands, which has remained unchanged for a thousand years...
>
> It is a soft and musical inflection, slightly melancholy, but companionable, the voice of people who are accustomed to hours of talking in the long winter evenings and do not feel they have to hurry; a splendid voice for telling stories in."

Norn the Language of Orkney

> "I am fifty years of age. When I was young, about five or six old men spoke mostly Norse but they were never taught to read or write any of it for a long time before so that their words and what does remain can be imperfect."

For almost 1,000 years, the language of the people of Orkney was a variant of Old Norse known as Norrœna, or Norn.

Originally carried to the Northern Isles by Norwegian settlers in the 8th and 9th centuries AD, their language, Old Norse, gradually developed into the distinctive language we now refer to as Norn.

The sheer scale of the Norse settlement of Orkney saw their language obliterate whatever indigenous language was spoken in Orkney. A few centuries later Norn was the dominant form of speech.

But unfortunately, because Norn was the language of the common people, it was never written down. Although official documents do exist from this period, they were generally written in Norwegian.

Norn remained the language of Orkney until the early 15th century, but, contrary to popular belief, its decline began well before the islands were annexed to Scotland, in 1468.

For many years prior to the impignoration, Scottish influence on Orkney had been on the increase. The Earldom had passed from Norwegian hands into Scottish ones and the influence of these Scottish earls must have had some effect on the "nobility" of Orkney.

Of particular importance, though, was the effect of Scotland on the church. Although the bishopric of Orkney was still subject to Norway, its bishops had shown a tendency to follow Scottish practices.

By 1312, the Scots calendar had been adopted and, as the clergy formed the bulk of the literate population of the island, the Scots language soon became more commonly used in clerical circles. This is clearly apparent when we note that the last official document written in Norwegian in Orkney appeared in 1445 23 years before King Christian I pawned the islands to raise cash for his daughter's dowry.

However, despite this growing "Scottification", it is likely that Orkney's rural population was largely unaffected and that the Scottish influence was restricted to the islands' upper classes. Because of this, Norn remained spoken in rural areas for 300 years or so later.

From the late 1500s to the early 1700s, most Orcadians were probably bilingual speaking both Norn and Scots English. But gradually, cultural change in society, coupled with the economic changes, meant that the old tongue began to die out.

By the early 19th century, only a handful of older Orcadians still knew the language. When they died, Norn went with them. Although Orcadians had spoken Norn for almost a millennium, few, if any, of them wrote or could write a word of it. The illiteracy of the general population meant that the exact form of the language is unknown with only a few tiny fragments of written Norn remaining to us today.

But although the grammar and intricacies of Norn are now lost, a huge number of Norn words survived in the spoken dialect of Orkney. These words, generally relating to everyday life, remained in the following centuries.

Orkney's 'Teu Neems'

The inhabitants of each district in Orkney have their own "teu-neem" or nickname.

Local tradition has it that the nicknames stem from the time of the construction of the St Magnus Cathedral.

They were allocated, it is said, depending upon the provisions the individual detachments of workers brought with them to Kirkwall.

Thus, Papay folk are known as Dundies, the Westray people as Auks.

It is doubtful that this tradition has any basis in truth, as similar nicknames are found in Shetland.

Whatever the origin, from the account of Jo Ben, we can see that at least two existed in the 16th century, and had probably been around for some time before that.

In some cases the teu-neems refer to animals, or birds, particular to the area, for example Hoy Hawks, while others seem to hint at the diets of the specific areas..

Others simply poke fun at, or insult, the parish inhabitants of the unfortunate parishes. All but a few of the teu-names are forgotten these days.

Orkney Placenames

An introduction
*"So the message is this: correct a wrong pronunciation when you hear it, demolish a false etymology when you can, and resist further attempts to anglicise these peculiar but splendid old names"*There is nothing that betrays Orkney's Norse heritage more than the islands' placenames.

In the eighth and ninth centuries AD, when the Norwegian settlers began arriving in Orkney, their placenames supplanted any original names. Because of this Orkney's placenames are now practically all Norse in origin. According to scholars there are over ten thousand of them, the majority of which are derivatives or corruptions of original Old Norse names. These old Norwegian words are found mingled with a few die-hard words of Celtic origin and a handful of later Scottish imports.

Placenames, even if used only for a short time, have a habit of sticking. This is certainly the case in Orkney.

Although the standardised spellings of many places in Orkney have been known to change over time, more often than not they retain their "correct" Orcadian pronunciation. Because of this, and also because of the whims of cartographers and historians throughout the centuries, to discern the root of any particular Orcadian placename it is usually best to listen to the way it is pronounced by an Orcadian, rather than go by its spelling on a map.

Our placenames have suffered greatly over the ages from the blundering of these map makers who knew nothing of Norn, the variant of Norse spoken in the islands.

Whenever they encountered a word that bore any resemblance to an English or Scottish word, it was common practice to immediately change it into what they assumed had to be its correct "English" form.

A classic example of this is Kirkwall. Originally pronounced "Kirkwaa", the name of the town derived from "Kirkvoe", which in turn came from "Kirkjuvagr" meaning "The Church Bay".

However, the early cartographers assumed that because the sound of the Orcadian -waa element was the same as the Scottish pronunciation of "wall" it had to mean the same. They promptly anglicised it and in one stroke "Kirkwaa" became "Kirkwall".

Unfortunately this distortion of placenames did not end with the early mapmakers but it is a process goes on today.

With many of the islands now housing more incomers than Orcadians, slowly but surely the ancient placenames of Orkney are being altered to suit these unfamiliar tongues.

Other Traditions

Eynhallow The Holy Isle

Away from the archaeology, Eynhallow, had, and still has, an important place in the traditions and folklore of Orkney.

From the accounts of Jo Ben, allegedly written in 1529, through to the "vanishing tourists" in 1990, the island remains steeped in "magic".

Buffeted by wind and wave, the Eynhallow of Orcadian tradition was an otherworldly place of sea-monsters and magic, appearing and disappearing out of the shifting mists until mortal man finally claimed it.

But Jo Ben, in his *Descriptio Insularum Orchadiarum*, was keen to stress to his readers that he did not believe in such "fabulous traditions".

He wrote:

"It is of old times related that here, if the standing corn be cut down, after the setting of the sun, unexpectedly there is a flowing of blood from the stalks of the grain; also it is said that if a horse is fastened, after sun-down it will easily get loose and wander anywhere during the night."

"Here you may discern the futitious and fabulous traditions of these people."

Eynhallow, the island of the Finfolk, where no rat, cat or mouse could thrive. An isle captured from these preternatural beings by an Evie farmer out for revenge.

The Guidman o' Thorodale seized the island, one of Orkney's two legendary vanishing isles, after a Finman abducted his wife. Aided by his sons, Thorodale cut nine crosses in Eynhallow's soil and circled its shore three times, sowing nine rings of salt.

"And so the Finfolk's Hildaland was cleared of all enchantment and lay bare. Empty and clean to the sight of man and heaven. Then it was called Eynhallow the Holy Isle and a church was raised there."

On this otherworldly place, surely there was no better place for an ecclesiastical settlement isolated by the raging roosts that spawned the Orcadian rhyme:

Eynhallow fair, Eynhallow free
Eynhallow sits in the middle o' the sea
A roaring roost on every side,
Eynhallow sits in the middle o' the tide.

Kelp Burning in Orkney

The burning of seaweed to make kelp was carried out in Orkney from the early 18th century until the early years of the 19th, at which time the industry went into decline.

The shallow waters surrounding Orkney, the sloping beaches and tremendous sea storms made the islands an ideal place to harvest kelp.

Tremendous quantities of tang and ware are washed ashore after the gales that regularly batter the islands, and these were easily gathered up, ready to be burned.

Seaweed had long been gathered by Orcadians, dragged up from the beaches and spread across the fields as a fertiliser.

This tradition was capitalised on by the island lairds, who quickly saw there were profits to be made gathering the seaweed and using it to produce kelp. The ash produced was rich in potash and soda, substances eagerly sought after by the glass and soap industries of the time.

The seaweed was gathered from the shores and laid out to dry, well above the high water mark. The piles of tang were then burned in large, stone-lined pits until the white powdery kelp was all that remained. The remains of kelp pits can be seen clearly today, across many of the north isles.

The remains of a series of kelp pits at the Ness o' Brough in Sanday.

Each kelp fire burned from four to eight hours, assisted by quantities of heather and hay.

The fire was watched constantly by the womenfolk, who ensured it was kept burning steadily. When the blaze was going well, the menfolk would pound the seaweed in the fire, before covering it with stones and turf and leaving it overnight.

The next morning, the chunks of kelp ash were cool enough to be broken into lumps and transported south.

The Orcadian crofters toiled at kelp burning between the months of June and August to subsidise their work on the land.

Undoubtedly hard and backbreaking work, the kelp industry not only caused the health of the workers to suffer but in later years the land became neglected because the lairds had all the islanders working at the kelp.

Stronsay was the first of Orkney's islands to start burning kelp, possibly as early as 1719, when the island's laird James Fea of Whitehall brought the practice to the island

To help, Fea brought a Scotsman named Meldrum to Orkney. This Meldrum was supposedly well-versed in the kelp production but it turned out he was something of a charlatan.

Eager to make the most of his position, Meldrum tried to convince the locals that only he knew the "magic words" and had enough of the "magic powder" to make the seaweed burn thoroughly.

Although superstitious, the Orcadians were no fools and paid little heed to Meldrum's wild claims.

Before long, the islands had a thriving kelp industry but its establishment was not without some protest. The opponents of kelp burning claimed that their livestock were being poisoned after inhaling the smoke blowing in from the shore. They even claimed that the limpets on the rocks were dying from the fumes and that the stench was driving away the fish.

The 50 or so years between 1780 and 1830 were Orkney's most profitable, with over 3,000 tones of kelp exported per annum.

The lairds gained most from this, retaining about three quarters of the selling price. Unfortunately, very little of this profit made its way back to the workers.

Kelp burning's death knell was sounded in the early 1800s when the discovery of mineral deposits in Germany crippled the industry and it went into decline.

Darraðarljoð The Battle Song of the Valkyries

According to *Njal's Saga*, on the morning of the Battle of Clontarf, a Caithness man, named Dörruðr (Daurrud), watched the "choosers of the slain" the Valkyries as they worked on a grisly loom, on which they controlled the fates of the armies in far off Ireland.

Their song, known as *Darraðarljoð*, was still recited in the Norn language in North Ronaldsay in the late eighteenth century.

"On Good-Friday that event happened in Caithness that a man whose name was Daurrud went out.

He saw folk riding twelve together to a bower, and there they were all lost to his sight.

He went to that bower and looked in through a window slit that was in it, and saw that there were women inside, and they had set up a loom.

Men's heads were the weights, but men's entrails were the warp and weft, a sword was the shuttle, and the reels were arrows. They sang these songs, and he learnt them by heart:

"See! warp is stretched
For warriors' fall,
Lo! weft in loom

'Tis wet with blood;
Now fight foreboding,
'Neath friends' swift fingers,
Our grey woof waxeth
With war's alarms,
Our warp bloodred,
Our weft corseblue.

"This woof is y-woven
With entrails of men,
This warp is hardweighted
With heads of the slain,
Spears blood-besprinkled
For spindles we use,
Our loom ironbound,

And arrows our reels;
With swords for our shuttles
This war-woof we work;
So weave we, weird sisters,
Our warwinning woof.

"Now Warwinner walketh
To weave in her turn,
Now Swordswinger steppeth,
Now Swiftstroke, now Storm;
When they speed the shuttle
How spearheads shall flash!
Shields crash, and helmgnawer
On harness bite hard!

"Wind we, wind swiftly
Our warwinning woof
Woof erst for king youthful
Foredoomed as his own,
Forth now we will ride,
Then through the ranks rushing
Be busy where friends
Blows blithe give and take.

"Wind we, wind swiftly
Our warwinning woof,
After that let us steadfastly
Stand by the brave king;
Then men shall mark mournful
Their shields red with gore,
How Swordstroke and Spearthrust
Stood stout by the prince.

"Wind we, wind swiftly
Our warwinning woof.
When sword-bearing rovers

Orkney

To banners rush on,
Mind, maidens, we spare not
One life in the fray!
We corse-choosing sisters
Have charge of the slain.

"Now new-coming nations
That island shall rule,
Who on outlying headlands
Abode ere the fight;
I say that King mighty
To death now is done,
Now low before spearpoint
That Earl bows his head.

"Soon over all Ersemen
Sharp sorrow shall fall,
That woe to those warriors
Shall wane nevermore;
Our woof now is woven.
Now battlefield waste,
O'er land and o'er water
War tidings shall leap.

"Now surely 'tis gruesome
To gaze all around.
When bloodred through heaven
Drives cloudrack o'er head;
Air soon shall be deep hued
With dying men's blood
When this our spaedom
Comes speedy to pass.

"So cheerily chant we
Charms for the young king,
Come maidens lift loudly

His warwinning lay;
Let him who now listens
Learn well with his ears
And gladden brave swordsmen
With bursts of war's song.

"Now mount we our horses,
Now bare we our brands,
Now haste we hard, maidens,
Hence far, far, away."

Then they plucked down the woof and tore it asunder, and each kept what she had hold of.

Now Daurrud goes away from the slit, and home; but they got on their steeds and rode six to the south, and the other six to the north. A like event befell Brand Gneisti's son in the Faroe Isles."

Orkney and the Arthurian Legends

There is one corpus of myth surrounding Orkney that most inhabitants of the county are generally ignorant of.

But this lore, although having Orkney at its centre, is not found in any shape or form within the culture or traditions of the islands.

It surprises many to learn of the major role played by Orkney in the legends and literature of King Arthur, the legendary British king who is supposed to have held back the Saxon advances in the 6th century AD.

At the core of the Arthurian mythos is a group of characters known as the Orkney Clan King Lot of Orkney and his sons, Gawain, Gaheris, Gareth, and Agravaine. Arthur's sister Morgause was married to King Lot.

Before we look at the origin of this material, we should recap the tale of King Arthur a story of magic, chivalry and betrayal.

The main Arthurian tale is well known how the boy Arthur draws the sword from the stone to become king; how he sets up the fabled Round Table in Camelot and receives the magical sword, Excalibur. Arthur's downfall is ultimately brought about by his son, Mordred, a child he fathered on his own sister, Morgause of Orkney.

Around this central theme are woven a number of sub-plots and stories involving the other members of the Orkney clan, in particular Gawain, one of the best-known knights of the Round Table, and Agravaine.

The Orkney clan

But although the Orkney clan feature heavily in the best-known legends of King Arthur, these stories were actually written around 1470.

Sir Thomas Malory's *Le Morte Darthur* is a piece of medieval fiction, although it could be argued that the story does contain heavily-veiled historical and cultural references.

Writing in the 15th century, Malory was the latest in a long list of author's who had adapted and expanded the Arthurian Legends to fit their own ideas. It is within Malory that the Orkney clan first appear and the islands have any sort of prominence within the Matter of Britain.

The development of the Arthurian Legends, from the first pseudo-historical sources to the tales of high chivalry of the Middle Ages is beyond the scope of this short article, but the reader can select from the links on the right for further information.

Suffice to say *Le Morte Darthur* was just one in a long line of retellings and adaptation of the Arthurian mythology. Prior to Malory, there was no Orkney clan and the Arthurian literature had only a few vague mentions of Orkney, which had no major part in the story.

It would be quite safe to say Malory's Orkney connection was a literary creations from the Middle Ages.

The Orkney connections

So is there any real historical link between the Arthurian legends and Orkney?

In short, no although we should remember that any traditions surrounding a Dark Ages king, or warrior, in Orkney could have been obliterated after the Norse takeover.

Over the years a number of hypothesis have been proposed as to the historical figure behind the Arthur of legend. A number of these theories have tantalising links to the islands, but these are generally refer to vague historical accounts of conquests or battles.

So, if there was any fabled connection between Orkney and a historical prototype on which the later Arthurian legends are based, it is now lost.

The Eternal Battle

The island of Hoy is said to be have once been the site of a magical battle. This bloody conflict was between the armies of two men and each night, after the bloodshed, the dead were reborn.

The battle was between the kings Högni, and Hedinn Hjarrandason.

Hedinn Hjarrandason had abducted King Högni's daughter, Hild, while the king was absent from his kingdom.

Upon his return Högni was enraged and, gathering his forces, set out in pursuit of Hedinn. Arriving in Norway Högni learned that Hedinn had sailed west over the sea towards Orkney.

Högni set of in pursuit and found Hedinn, and Hild, in Hoy.

Hild, who had since married Hedinn, tried to make peace between her father, offering him a necklace on behalf of her new husband.

She begged him to avoid conflict, saying that Hedinn was ready to fight, and if it came to battle, the old king could expect no mercy at her husband's hand.

But the old king had been insulted and sought battle. So he ignored his daughter's pleas.

Saddened, Hild returned to Hedinn and told him there would be no reconciliation. The warriors prepared to fight.

When the two armies deployed for battle, Hedinn once again tried to make peace, offering the king a fortune in gold in order to prevent war. But it was not enough.

Högni, who had unsheathed his sword, Dáinsleif, said the peace offering was too late.

"Your offer of peace comes too late, " said Högni. "My blade has been drawn. Forged by the dwarves it cannot be sheathed until it has drawn blood or taken life."

Hedinn glared at the old man.

"You can boast about your sword, but victory will not be yours. I call any sword good which is faithful to its master."

So the bloodshed began.

The two armies fought fiercely until nightfall, when the survivors from both sides retired to their camps, leaving a battlefield strewn with the dead of both sides.

As the moon crept above the horizon, Hild walked among the fallen, and with her magic, brought the slain back to life, ready to fight the same battle the next morning.

By the time the sun arose, those who had fallen the day before had joined their comrades, ready to resume battle.

Once again, the two sides met fiercely and the field was reddened with blood.

The arrival of night once again ended the conflict and, once again, Hild used her magic to revive the fallen so that they might rise again to fight the same battle.

Thus the cycle continued.

The two armies fought during the day, and at night the dead were resurrected. They rose again in the morning and gathered their weapons and shields, which had turned to stone overnight, to fight another day.

Tradition has it that the two armies were cursed to fight one another until the day of Ragnarok.

Odin in Orkney tradition

References to the Norse god Odin abound throughout Orkney folklore, tradition and even the landscape.

In Norse mythology, Odin was the most powerful of all the gods. Known as Allfather, Odin was generally depicted as an old, long-bearded, one-eyed man, wearing a cloak and wide-brimmed hat.

Orkney has numerous placenames that are thought to stem to Odin, places such as Odinsgarth, Odiness and Otterswick a corruption of the original name Odinswick. However, when it comes to placenames, caution must be employed as many can be ascribed to the personal names, Audun or Oddi.

Perhaps the most famous of the Odin landmarks was the revered Odin Stone in the Mainland parish of Stenness.

This holed monolith was the focus of the unbreakable "Aith o' Odin". The potency of this Stone o' Odin, as well as the oath, was considerable and remained in common use until the stone's destruction in 1814.

Although the words to the Odin Oath have been lost, transmitted as they were orally down the generations, an ancient Orkney poem, the *Play o' da Lathie Odivere* leaves us in no doubt as to Odin's involvement, referring as it does to "him dat hanged on da tree."

This vague sentence refers to the episode in Norse mythology in which Odin sacrifices himself on Ygdrassil, the world tree, to gain the knowledge of life, death and runes.

For nine days and nights he hung, suspended upside down, impaled by his spear, Gungnir.

This episode is remembered in the folk-rhyme:

> *Nine lang nichts i' da nippin rime,*
> *Hange he dare wi' naked limb*

As well as his role as oath-god, the one-eyed deity was also regarded by the Norse as the gatherer of souls, and to this end was responsible for leading the Wild Hunt on its nightime rampages across the sky.

No specific remnants of this tradition, found throughout Britain and Europe, is remembered in Orkney, although a few scattered tales of spectral black hounds may have some connection to this one-time widespread belief.

A well-known charm used in the northern isles for curing sprains clearly points at Norse heathenism. Although overlain at some point with Christian reference, the charm is an exact duplicate of the one used by Odin to heal the god Balder's horse. Click here for more details.

There are also certain veiled connections to Odin within certain Orcadian harvest traditions.

Magnus the Martyr of Orkney

The resting places of Magnus' body

Local tradition has it that the body of St Magnus, en route from Evie to Birsay for its burial, was rested at a number of places.

Key to these beliefs were the customs surrounding wheelie-stanes. These were ingrained into Orkney's funerary customs.

At a time when transporting a corpse to its final resting place meant a considerable trek, all the while carrying a body or coffin, it was considered unlucky to set down the body, or coffin, anywhere except specific traditional spots along the route.

These stopping-points were known as *wheelie kros* or *wheelie stanes*, a name deriving from the Norse word *hvila* meaning *to rest*.

The origin of these points, and why they were considered suitable, is unclear but it has been suggested they may once have been the sites of roadside shrines. Others were undoubtedly places of ancient, pagan significance wells, stones etc.

Writing in *The Orcadian* in 1972, Ernest Marwick noted that, according to a Birsay resident, the traditional wheelie-places for St Magnus' corpse were:

- ✓ Mans Stone
- ✓ Lingro
- ✓ Crustan
- ✓ Waspitten
- ✓ A stone in a field near Skippigeo/Skibbageo.

He wrote:

"*If Lingro to Crustan was a stage between rests, and Waspitten to Skippigeo another, there must have been intermediate stages between Mans Stone and Lingro and Crustan and Waspitten.*

"The high lands of Costa Hill and Crustan behind them, the bearers took the comparatively easy path along the shore between Crustan and Waspitten.

"Waspitten was a stone on a field on the farm of Doverhouse, formerly called Flecketsquoy. A strip of land on which the stone lay was never ploughed: it was sacred ground as the body of the saint had rested there."

During the Second World War, however, service men from the nearby military camp had other views about the stone they broke it up to make concrete.

The Westray Dons and the Spanish Armada

There can be few people who don't know the story of the English nobleman, Sir Francis Drake, and the Spanish Armada.

When the Armada was sighted on July 19, 1588, Drake was playing a game of bowls on Plymouth Hoe in England. Legend has it that he finished his game boarding his vessel, the *Revenge*.

But although this historical tale of the Spanish Armada is well-known, few outside Orkney know the historical impact the Armada had on the islands.

After Drake had foiled the invading Armada, the remnants of the crippled Spanish fleet were scattered into the North Sea. With the English vessels in pursuit, the Spanish Admiral of the Fleet ordered his ships to run for home, crossing the north of the British Isles, before limping homeward through the Atlantic.

But not all the Armada ships made it past the Northern Isles.

Writing in 1889, the Orkney antiquarian and folklorist, Walter Traill Dennison, of West Brough, Sanday, recorded the fate of some of these ships.

In a paper he wrote for the Orkney Natural History Society, he recited a number of oral traditions "gathered from the lips of old people."

Wrecked on the Fair Isle

Among these was the loss of the Armada flagship, *El Gran Grifon*, commanded by the Admiral, The Duke of Medina, which was wrecked on the Fair Isle, the island between Orkney and Shetland.

According to historian, Sir Robert Sibbald, the islanders had, at first, kindly entertained the crew but, as winter approached, they feared the extra population would quickly exhaust food supplies, causing everyone to starve.

But although the Spaniards have been paying well for all they received, a Fair Isle man, relating the tail to Traill Dennison, said: "Spanish money couldna' fill hungry bellies".

Accordingly, wrote Traill Dennison, the islanders threw any unfortunate Spaniard, found alone, over the cliffs. Then a quicker plan was devised the islanders deliberately collapsed the flagstone roof of the dwelling where Spaniards were sleeping.

The surviving Spaniards, including the Duke of Medina, then fled to Shetland. Here, the Duke enjoyed the hospitality of a Shetland laird who, it seems, later arranged his repatriation as far as Dunkirk.

Westray hospitality

However, if the hospitality of the Fair Isle's inhabitants left something to be desired, the folk of Westray more than compensated. Here, they were offered sanctuary, with a number not only settling on the island, but also marrying and beginning a unique community, vestiges of which survives today.

These Spanish settlers, and their descendants, became renowned as daring seafarers and notorious smugglers.

The Spanish seamen found themselves in Westray after a ship was wrecked in the fierce water of Dennis Rost, off North Ronaldsay. The surviving crewmen, who had taken to the lifeboats, then made their way to Westray looking for a safe place to make landfall.

The came ashore at Pierowall, thereafter, according to Traill Dennison, they:

> "seem to have taken kindly to the island, where they built houses for themselves, married wives and formed a little settlement by themselves on what is called the North Shore.

> "After the first union by marriage of the Spaniards with Orcadian females, none of the race were allowed to marry with any but the descendants of the original settlers, and their descendants have since been termed Dons.

> "These Dons seem to have kept themselves strictly from intermarrying with the rest of the people for a time.

> "The Dons seem to have adopted in most cases Orkney names. Among their principal names were Petrie, Reid and Hewison. Though their descendants in some cases can still be traced, the Dons, as a separate caste, no longer exist."

Traill Dennison's own grandfather, who lived at Noltland Castle, and who, in the summer months, traded with Continental ports, used to teach navigation and nautical skills to the young men of Westray.

He wrote: "During a pretty long life, he taught the nautical science to 140 young men, 80 per cent of whom are said to have been Dons."

"Most of these men left the county as sailors and many became sea captains," he added.

Apart from their proficiency as mariners, the Dons were also said to be fine actors who could entertain islanders with winter drama productions.

But although Traill Dennison had written that "the Dons, as a separate caste, no longer exist", he stressed that physical features remained that could still identify the descendants of the Armada survivors.

He wrote:

> *"The union of Spanish blood with the Norse produced a race of men active and daring; with dark eyes, and sometimes with features of a foreign caste; in manners fidgety and restless a true Don being rarely able to sit in one position for five minutes, unless he was dead drunk; and in conversation more demonstrative and more given to gesticulate than the true Orcadian; while ready in wit, and perpetrating a practical joke, he was far superior to the native race."*

The Stages of Life

Orcadian Childbirth Traditions

There was a time in Orkney, when childbirth was surrounded by superstition, uncertainty and, above all, fear.

Because of this, pregnancy and childbirth were surrounded by a number of spells, incantations, prohibitions and precautions a mixture of magic and religion aimed at protecting both mother and child.

The most common and deeply-rooted Orkney tradition was the absolute requirement to keep a pregnancy concealed. This was deemed necessary to avoid attracting the unwanted, and malicious, attention of either the trows or the fairy folk.

If these creatures were to learn of an impending birth, they would be sure to bring harm to both mother and unborn infant. Because of this, it was extremely unlucky to prepare for the coming of a new baby. Any such activity, it was thought, would alert the trows to the woman's condition.

Precautions taken against the influence of trows continued throughout pregnancy, reaching a peak with the birth of the child. In some accounts, the danger was only thought to pass after the child had cut its first tooth.

Iron and scriptures

Because of widespread fear of the trows and fairy folk, pregnant women were guarded continuously throughout the labour process.

For protection, a knife and Bible were placed in the bed beside her. The iron of the knife, together with the power of the holy scriptures, was a guaranteed deterrent to any supernatural interference.

Then, immediately after the infant's birth, both knife and Bible were transferred to the awaiting cradle. At the same time, the attention of the family switched to protecting the helpless child.

Following the arrival of the baby, it was customary for the women who had been present at the delivery to remain in the house for several days. These women were afforded the best food and drink the household could give them. In some recorded cases, as many as six women were known to remain in the house, their sole duty to protect the vulnerable child, and to a certain extent, the nursing mother, from the fairy folk.

As detailed in section dealing with the trows, if a child sickened or failed to thrive, it was declared that the protective measures had failed. The healthy young infant, it was often thought, had surely been spirited away, replaced by a sickly changeling.

"Weetin' the heed"

One tradition that followed an Orcadian birth remains strong today.

"Weetin' the heed o' the bern", or Wetting the child's head, was an inescapable custom that ensured the infant was brought luck.

A bottle of whisky was brought out for the occasion and hastily consumed by the new father and the menfolk of the area.

It was also not uncommon for the child's first drink to be from this bottle. A drop of whisky regarded as "an infallible cure for all infantile ailments" was immediately fed to the baby with a teaspoon.

To ensure the infant's good luck, it was preferable that this be a silver teaspoon. However, as most households could not afford this luxury, a silver coin, very often borrowed, was placed in the spoon and was thought to suffice. Silver, in the form of a coin, is still given to newborn infants.

The reliance on alcohol during childbirth was recorded by local author John Firth. Writing his reminiscences in 1920, the 82-year-old Firth remarked:

"It was no uncommon occurrence at an accouchement for the mother and all her attendants to be the worse of drink...what with the want of skill, and the superstitious customs and drunkenness, it is surprising that more precious lives were lost."

The newborn's 'Blide Maet'

Like marriage, the birth of an Orcadian child was celebrated with a number of specific feasts.

The first of these, known as the "blide-maet" (joy-food), was served to visiting family and neighbours who called to view the baby and congratulate the mother. The blide-maet was passed out at regular intervals and usually consisted of scones and ale.

During these visits, it was considered very unwise to audibly praise or admire the infant without first saying "Geud save hid" (God save it) or "Sef bae hid" (Safe be it). Without these precautions against supernatural attention, the child was said to be "forespoken" almost confirming that it was too good to live.

Little is remembered of the second feast the "Fittin' Feast".

It is likely that it did exist across Orkney, but in communities that recorded little, it has since been forgotten.

What we do know of the "Fittin' Feast" is that it was a private meal for the child's immediate family and marked the mother's return "to the fire" the time when she was able to resume her daily household duties.

Christening the infant

The third and final feast was the "Cirsenin' Feast".

Celebrated immediately after the baptism, this generally took place within two weeks of the birth, but more often within the first week.

It should be remembered that any Orkney child that died without being christened could not be buried in the consecrated ground of the kirkyard. In an age where infant mortality was high, christening was considered, unsurprisingly, a priority.

When it comes to Christenings, one peculiar tradition was that male children had to be baptised first.

If not, and a female was the first to receive the Holy Water, the young girl was doomed to grow a beard, while the boys would remain beardless.

Marriage Divinations

As is mentioned, briefly, in the section dealing with Orcadian wedding traditions, in bygone days a young Orcadian girl, growing up on a croft, or farm, had but two prospects in life.

She could marry, start a home and family, or remain with her parents, a spinster, spending her days looking after the family home.

Needless to say, marriage was high on the list of priorities of most Orcadian girls. It was therefore imperative that they attract and secure a husband.

A classic example of the seriousness with which the Orcadian women regarded marriage is the superstition that it was considered extremely dangerous to let water boil alone in a pot. If this occurred, it was a certainty that the girls within that household would lose their sweethearts. This tradition also serves to indicate the importance placed on superstition in everyday Orcadian life.

The road to marriage may have been rocky but these young ladies were not content to sit and wait for fate to deal its cards. From her earliest days an Orcadian girl took part in numerous forms of divination with the sole intention of finding out any tiny snippet of information relating to her future love.

In most cases the results of these divinations appear to the modern reader as insignificant the anxious girl could perhaps hope to discover the colour of her the lover's hair, the sound of his voice or perhaps the direction in which he lived. All seemingly pointless and general information.

But with all these we must remember that in small island communities where everyone knew everyone else, the diviner was almost certain to know someone who, in some way, fitted the results. In a land steeped in superstition and lore, could we go as far as saying the idea planted within a maiden's head after her divinations may have been the catalyst in more than a few courtships or marriages?

Across the islands it was generally agreed that there were certain times of the year when an attempt to peer through the veil into the future was likely to be successful.

Traditionally these times were Candlemas (2 February), Johnsmas (Midsummer) and the most commonly used Halloween (31 October).

The forms these divinations took were varied and the methods employed also differed from isle to isle and parish to parish. Some were little more than vague interpretations of natural occurrences while others had stricter almost ritualistic procedures that had to be adhered to. The latter group usually resulted in a "conjured" up a likeness of the future husband.

These divinations existed as oral lore and as such few were actually recorded. Some examples from the former category are:

- At Candlemas each year, the girl should startle the first crow she saw. The direction in which the bird flew was the direction in which her future husband lived. If the panicked bird flew over a churchyard, the girl was certain to remain a spinster.
- Flowers picked from Ribwort Plantain were placed under a stone. If the plant grew more flowers before the heads under the stone withered, the girl and her sweetheart were sure to marry.
- Sweethearts would place two straws one for each of them and named accordingly onto a glowing peat. A knot had been tied on one of the straws and the heat within the peat would eventually cause this straw to jump. If the straw leapt toward the other it was a sure sign that the sweethearts would marry.
- On the Orkney mainland, one tradition recorded within the parish of Orphir has the girl removing a burning coal from the fire and extinguishing it in a bucket of water. The coal was then placed under a turf and left. When the next morning dawned, the turf was broken in two and examined. If a hair was found, it was sure to be the same colour as her future husband's.
- After the bonfire festivities, girls often carried home a partially burned peat which would be completely extinguished in a tub of "strang bing" (urine) and placed on the door lintel. The peat would be taken down the next day, broken in two and the colour of the peat within would foretell the colour of the girl's future husband.

The second category are by far the more interesting. Most of the rituals within this group were specifically carried out at Halloween and may hark back to a common Orcadian belief that all living people had a "ganfer" a supernatural duplicate or "doppleganger".

For a person to meet there own "ganfer" was disastrous for it meant certain death but in these cases they merely allowed the girl to glimpse the form of her intended. For more on the ganfer

- The most common of the Halloween divinations involved the sieve, the scissors and the knife. The brave girl would leave the house and go to the barn (or other building) where she had to stand in the dark, winnowing "three wechts o naitheen" with the sieve containing the knife and the scissors. If carried out correctly, the girl could expect to see an apparition of her future husband pass the open door.
- A similar ritual had the hopeful young girl hanging a wetted sleeve in front of the fire before retiring to bed. Once in bed she would wait for an apparition of her future spouse to enter her room and "turn the shift".
- A salt herring, eaten before bedtime, would ensure a visitation by the husband-to-be, who would appear sometime during the night to quench the girl's thirst with a draught of cold water.
- In order to hear the voice of their future love, the girl in question had to throw a ball of "worsted" (wool) into the kiln used for drying grain, while reciting:

  "Wha taks had o me clew's end"

  The disembodied voice that answered (if any) was said to be that of the girl's husband. Needless to say, this ritual was the source of numerous japes in and around farms, when local lads would hide themselves within the kiln awaiting the arrival of the anxious maidens.
- A final example regarding the spectre of a future love involved the young lass entering the farm's stackyard at night, running round its circumference with her arms outstretched. Upon reaching full circle she would embrace the apparition of an unknown man the man she was destined to wed.

Orcadian Wedding Traditions

Customs and First Steps

The typical Orcadian wedding was, and to a certain extent still is, much more than a simple family affair.

A wedding was a time to celebrate a time to break free from the rigours of daily life and participate in an event that could last for days, and involved the entire community.

Speirin night'

The first stage of the old Orcadian wedding traditions took place on the night on which the prospective groom formally asked his sweetheart's father for her hand in marriage.

This night was referred to as "speirin' night", from the dialect word *speir* meaning *to ask*.

On this quest it was common for the hopeful lad to carry a bottle of whisky, which was known as the speirin' bottle. With this liquor he would hope to sway the father's decision in his favour. Then, if permission was granted, tentative arrangements were discussed over a few glasses from the speiring bottle.

Orcadian Wedding Traditions

The Wedding Cogs

At an Orkney wedding feast, ale was consumed from wooden vessels known as cogs.

These cogs were undoubtedly the most essential of all the ingredients that made up an old island wedding.

The cog is simply a circular drinking vessel. Hand-crafted from wood, it is formed from staves held securely by wooden or metal hoops. Two or three long upright handles rise from the brim of the vessel allowing the bride and the groom to carry the cog around from guest to guest.

Traditionally the cogs at each wedding feast were divided into two distinct types. These were the menye-cogs and the cog-gilt-cogs.

The cog-gilt-cogs were confined to each individual cog-gilt a cog-gilt being the large table that sat 24 guests. The menye-cogs, on the other hand, were passed throughout the wedding hall and drunk from by the assembled guests. Menye-cogs had a distinctive appearance, with every alternate stave made of a dark wood, thus giving them a variegated appearance.

Of the menye-cogs, three types were circulated at each wedding the "geud-man's cog" (the Best Man's Cog), the "priest's cog" and the "bride's cog".

The tradition of the menye-cogs survives today, although only the geud-man's cog and the bride's cog are found in common use.

Originally, the geud-man's cog was the first to be passed around and began with the bride's father. The priest's cog, or grace-cup as it was sometimes known, followed the wedding meal. Once the priest had supped from this cog, and toasted the married couple, it was handed to the neighbour at his left hand side.

Like many aspects of Orcadian tradition, it was always considered essential that the cog only move around the room "sunwise", in accordance to the motion of the sun.

In bygone days, it was common for a typical Orkney wedding to last all night, if not well into the next day. The third menye-cog, the bride's cog, was the last to make an appearance and was brought out in the early hours of the morning.

Shortly after the late supper, preparations were made for the brew that filled the bride's cog. This concoction was made up of a mixture of hot ale, gin, brandy and whisky which was then mixed with some eggs.

The bride had to be the first to drink from the bride's cog, before it was passed to all present and replenished with the warm liquor as and when required. Few of those still sober from the night's earlier drinking were rarely able to consume much of the cog without becoming quickly and completely drunk.

The exact mixture which now goes into the cog varies with every wedding, as each family tends to have its own views on the correct recipe. Despite the family variations, the base ingredients of this potent alcoholic mixture are usually hot ale, gin, brandy and whisky mixed with sugar and pepper.

Apart from the Grand March a later variant of the old Wedding Walk the sharing of the Bride's Cog is the only one of the old ceremonies still found at Orcadian weddings today.

The Customs of Death

Omens of an impending death

Death, like birth and marriage, is a major rite of passage and, in Orkney, was regarded as a time when the living were vulnerable to the influences of the supernatural.

Here, the fears surrounding death were allayed somewhat by an elaborate series of rituals and customs.

These not only protected the living from the dead but, in some cases, ensured the spirits of the deceased moved safely from this world to the next.

In Orkney, the relationship between the dead and the living was ambivalent, varying from minor concern to mortal terror. In most cases, however, fear was the driving emotion.

The power of the deceased's spirit was greatly feared, in particular that it might return to plague the household as a ghost.

This might seem contrary to the anxieties surrounding birth and marriage, when the trows were the main objects of terror, but in truth I believe them to be the same. As is discussed elsewhere on this site, I am firmly of the opinion that Orkney's trows originally represented the returning spirits of the dead.

With this driving fear of the unknown, and when surrounded by the dead of countless centuries, it was inevitable that the old Orcadians not only took steps to protect themselves, but also tried to foresee, and perhaps stall, the return of death to their households.

In those times, the fear and inevitability of death was something we can now barely comprehend.

The reaper waited patiently in the shadows and his chances were many.... a poor harvest, widespread illness or a fierce storm at sea all these, and more, provided the means for Death to claim yet another victim.

And if the unfortunate victim survived this time, Death was sure to have his chance again.

With this grim spectre ever present, signs that would give some clue as to when and where death would strike again were eagerly sought. All manner of events were thought to be omens of death. Climatic events, animals, noises, dreams and visions believed to foretell a death and reveal who would next be in the kirkyard.

As is common with much of Orcadian folk tradition, few customs surrounding death made it onto paper. This is probably for no other reason than the people of Orkney had no wish to share this knowledge with those who regarded them as superstitious or ignorant.

Foretelling doom

We do, however, have a few examples.

In much the same way that the appearance of a rainbow a *bifrit* in old Orcadian dialect could foretell the birth of a child, it could also be interpreted as an omen of death.

When both ends of a rainbow were contained within the dyke that encircled the tunship, it was declared that someone within would soon die.

"There's a brig for een oot o' da toon!" was the exclamation on this occasion.

The same idea applied when both ends of the rainbow were seen on an island.

Perhaps the most common death omen in Orcadian households was a clicking sound, described by some as like "the ticking of a clock or the dripping of water". This sound, usually explained away as the noise caused by woodworm, was regarded as a signal that a death in the household would follow.

Birds were also common precursors of death, a superstition that remained throughout my childhood and may well still exist today.

In the Northern Isles, a number of birds could be omens of death, but the role fell particularly on the raven, crow or owl. Seeing either of these birds perched on a rooftop inevitably meant someone inside would soon pass away.

Staying with the birds, the unnatural sound of a cock crowing a midnight was another sign a belief that may have something to do with the motif of the vardenas was a flying birrd striking a window pane.

Death dreams and white kail

Regarding dreams, for example, a vision of a ship travelling on dry land was an omen of your death, while to dream of losing a tooth meant losing a friend or relative.

Perhaps the strangest of these notions was the idea that the appearance of a white cabbage within the house's kailyard (cabbage patch) was a certain sign of death.
This was said to bring forth the exclamation: "We'll soon be hearing dead news!"

www.ingramcontent.com/pod-product-compliance
Lightning Source LLC
Chambersburg PA
CBHW021058080526
44587CB00010B/292